OVERVIEW

Overview

You're likely to have gone through a day during which you experienced a range of emotions. But do you pay enough attention to these? If you've been taught to suppress your emotions or always to prioritize rational thought above what you feel, it can actually have negative consequences – for you personally, and even in a business context.

How in tune are you with the emotions in your life? In thinking about your answer to this, consider these basic questions:

- Do you let yourself feel strong emotions like anger or joy?
- Do you feel your emotions physically – for example, in your chest?
- Do you consider your emotions when making decisions or attempt to put them aside?
- Are you comfortable expressing your emotions to those around you?

- Do you recognize others' emotions, or do they escape your notice or simply not seem important enough to notice?

As you may have deduced, emotions can have enormous power. They can motivate you to act by steering you toward what you desire and away from what you find unpleasant. Even negative emotions like anger can be beneficial by providing you with a stimulus to take productive action.

Emotions also help you understand your needs and those of others.

And recognizing and taking them into account can help you build strong, healthy relationships and improve your ability to relate to others.

To live full, rewarding lives, people need to make use of their minds and their hearts. Intellect and emotion aren't opposed to each other – they work together, informing your perceptions and reactions.

Favoring one or the other throws things out of balance.

But it's not possible to use emotions to your advantage if you suppress or misinterpret them. So emotional awareness is vital. It involves accurately recognizing your emotions and those of others.

A person's emotional intelligence quotient – or EQ for short – is the capacity to reason about emotional information. EQ is increasingly recognized as important in both personal and work environments.

Even in business contexts, where rational thought is traditionally valued over emotional skills, research shows that EQ is an important predictor of success.

This applies especially in areas where dealing well with others is crucial, like sales. People with high EQs relate better to others, make better use of feedback to develop themselves, and generally possess greater understanding of their environments than those with low EQs.

EQ can be divided into four general areas of competence – self-awareness, self-management, empathy, and relationship management.

Read more about each competency area for more information about it.

Self-awareness

Self-awareness involves being aware of your own emotions, experiencing them, and understanding how they affect your actions and thoughts.

Self-management

Self-management involves controlling your emotions rather than allowing them to control you. This self-control is vital in dealing successfully with others and with challenges you face.

Empathy

Empathy involves understanding the emotional reactions of others, even if these differ from yours, and being able to view situations from others' points of view.

Relationship management

Relationship management covers the skills that enable you to deal well with others, and includes taking responsibility for your actions and their consequences.

In this book you'll learn about the power of emotions and the benefits of developing awareness of emotions in your daily life. You'll also learn to distinguish between the traits of people with high intelligence quotients – commonly know as IQ – and those with high EQs, and about the value of having a high EQ. Finally, you'll learn about the four emotional competency areas, and how to distinguish between them.

EQ is vital to success in both private and public spheres of life. Developing your EQ can sometimes be difficult, but can have enormous benefits. This book will teach you how to realize and harness the power of emotions and reap those benefits.

Intelligence doesn't relate only to how well you apply logic or the store of facts at your disposal. Having emotional intelligence is equally essential for personal and professional success.

Consider Doug, who's a middle manager in a large firm. He's a smart, shrewd businessman who knows his industry inside out. Although he's a fair boss, his employees dislike him. He comes across as cold and aloof, and struggles to interact with and "read" other people. He has always battled to handle stress, and after his wife is diagnosed with cancer, he collapses under the pressure and suffers a nervous breakdown.

Heather never went to college, but is a successful entrepreneur. She finds it easy to get along with others and her natural warmth draws people to her. Her sense of humor has always helped her weather stressful times. When her mother passes away, she doesn't let her grief overwhelm her. Instead, she finds the strength to stay positive and overcome her loss.

Question

Which person – Heather or Doug – do you think demonstrates a higher level of emotional intelligence?

Options:
1. Heather

2. Doug
Answer:
Option 1: This is the correct option. Heather may not be college educated, but she is "head smart." She knows how to read her own emotions and how to empathize with others – the cornerstones of emotional intelligence.

Option 2: This is an incorrect option. Doug may be an intelligent person, but intellectual intelligence isn't the same as emotional intelligence, which refers to how you manage your emotions.

Heather demonstrates a high EQ, which is short for "emotional intelligence quotient." This is the emotional counterpart of IQ, or "intelligence quotient." Society often places a higher value on IQ. But the truth is that your EQ is just as important a factor in your success.

Four key competency areas contribute to your EQ – self-awareness, self-management, empathy, and relationship management.

Review each competency area for more information about what it comprises.

Self-awareness

Self-awareness is the ability to look inward and to recognize your own strengths and weaknesses, what emotions you're experiencing, and how they affect you personally. It also involves recognizing triggers that set off certain emotional responses in you.

Self-management

Self-management is the ability to control your emotional reactions. You don't deny or try to suppress your feelings, but you know how to manage inappropriate emotional reactions so they don't get the better of you. Self-management relies on self-awareness.

Empathy

Another way to describe empathy is "social smarts." You're empathetic when you recognize and understand the emotions, needs, and concerns of other people. You pick up on the nonverbal cues others send out.

Relationship management

Relationship management is the ability to connect with others and to maintain good, healthy relationships with them. It's the ability to communicate your feelings, understand other perspectives, and handle conflict situations.

Each competency area pertains either to your own emotions or to the emotions of those around you. Each competency also pertains either to being aware of or managing those emotions. This book will focus on the competencies related to personal awareness and management – identifying and regulating your own emotions.

These competencies relate to one another. You can't recognize the emotions of others or manage your relationships effectively before you understand and can control your own emotions.

In this book, you'll learn various strategies for improving your self-awareness and self-management skills:

- the value of being self-aware, how to recognize different emotions, and techniques for developing your self-awareness,
- the value of self-management and the ability to control your emotional reactions, and
- various self-management techniques and how to apply them in your own life.

Often getting a job done requires objectivity and a focus on the facts. But this doesn't mean you and your colleagues must leave your emotions at the door when you enter the workplace.

Positive effects of managing emotions

Your emotions have significant effects on your work performance, decision making, and interactions with others. Being aware of the role of emotions in the workplace can help you manage both yourself and others far more effectively. This can result in better decisions, productivity, and teamwork.

Psychologist and author Daniel Goleman performed pioneering work when he identified key competency areas that make up a person's emotional intelligence quotient – commonly known as EQ. These include personal and social areas, related to both awareness and management. This course focuses on the social aspects of EQ – empathy and relationship management.

Revisit each social competency area for more information about it.

Empathy

Empathy is the ability to sense and understand the emotions of others. It's directly tied to social effectiveness, making it easier to solve or prevent problems and conflicts.

To show empathy, you need to identify and acknowledge others' emotions, suspend judgment, and demonstrate your availability and support.

Relationship management

Relationship management determines your ability to build positive, productive relationships and communicate effectively. You can do this well only if you have skills in three other competency areas that make up EQ – self-awareness, self-management, and empathy. In other words, you need to be able to recognize and manage your own emotions and those of others before you can build effective relationships.

This course focuses on the relationship management skills that are especially important in a work environment – those needed for teamwork, collaboration, and developing people.

Tina is an advertising copywriter. She needs a colleague, Thom, to check her ideas before she goes ahead with them. She's under a lot of pressure, but each time she goes to Thom's desk, he's away at a meeting. After her third attempt, Tina leaves an abrupt scrawled message on Thom's desk, with a time deadline.

When Thom returns, he's annoyed by the tone of Tina's note and decides to ignore her request until she comes to explain more clearly what she needs. He sends a rather unfriendly e-mail to Tina and carries on with his own tasks.

Both Tina and Thom fail to take emotional reactions into account, which affects their productivity and decision making.

If Tina and Thom had built their skills in detecting, leveraging, and managing emotions in the workplace, they both may have made better decisions. And they would have found a more productive way of working together. This course focuses on teaching you to do just that.

And, with this short example, we are ready to start the emotional intelligence exploration.

CHAPTER I - WHAT IS EMOTIONAL INTELLIGENCE

CHAPTER I - What is Emotional Intelligence?

In this chapter you'll learn about the power of emotions and the benefits of developing awareness of emotions in your daily life.

You'll also learn to distinguish between the traits of people with high intelligence quotients – commonly know as IQ – and those with high EQs, and about the value of having a high EQ. Finally, you'll learn about the four emotional competency areas, and how to distinguish between them.

EQ is vital to success in both private and public spheres of life. Developing your EQ can sometimes be difficult, but can have enormous benefits. This book will teach you how to realize and harness the power of emotions and reap those benefits.

THE POWER OF EMOTIONS

The power of emotions

Emotions have a powerful influence over thought. Perhaps you've had an experience similar to the following. While working late one night, Martin hears the sound of shattering glass. Is it an intruder? His heart beats faster and his senses are heightened as adrenaline pumps through his body. He walks carefully through the house, only to find his cat on a table – and an ornament lying broken on the floor below. Martin breathes a sigh of relief.

The incident evoked a number of strong emotions in Martin, including both intense fear and relief. These feelings, along with other emotions such as happiness, excitement, anger, and contentment, play crucial roles in our lives.

Emotions can be powerful allies. They can motivate you to take necessary action, help you understand your needs and those of other people, and help you build strong relationships with others.

See each function of emotions for more information.

Motivate action

Emotions, whether positive or negative, motivate you to take the necessary actions to meet your goals. They steer you toward what you desire or need, and away from what you find unpleasant.

Understand needs

When you're aware of your own emotions, it's easier for you to recognize what you need. Similarly, being aware of other people's emotions enables you to recognize what they need. This helps you to make effective decisions based on what's most important to you and others.

Build relationships

Emotions help you to connect with other people and build strong relationships. If you're not aware of others' emotions, you won't be able to relate to them effectively.

Emotions aren't purely in the mind. They manifest physically as well.

Think back to the example of Martin, who thought he heard an intruder. His fear triggered a chemical reaction, making his heart beat faster and more oxygen flow to his cells.

This is known as a "fight or flight" response. Emotions like intense fear or anger cause the human body to prepare itself, either to confront or flee a physical threat.

But "fight or flight" responses are not exclusive to possible physical confrontations. They can also occur in situations that aren't physically threatening.

For example, if a colleague disagrees with you very aggressively, your emotional response may be as intense as if you were confronted by a threat to your well being.

Although your instinctive physical reactions are to fight or flee, it's likely neither of these purely physical responses are appropriate. With mental control though, they could motivate you to take other actions – like defending yourself verbally or perhaps lodging a complaint with a manager.

Question

Anger and fear aren't the only emotions that can help you adapt to a situation you're facing.

Match examples of other emotions to descriptions of how they may benefit you in particular circumstances.

Options:

A. Worry
B. Surprise
C. Disgust
D. Happiness

Targets:

1. Prompts you to rehearse future scenarios and plan effective actions

2. Heightens your arousal and sensitivity to input

3. Enables you to avoid things that are repellent or noxious, or could harm you 4. Can inhibit negative feelings and motivate you

Answer:

Worry often prompts you to imagine future scenarios and play through their possible outcomes in your mind. This can help prepare you, enabling you to plan effective actions in case an event you've tackled mentally actually occurs.

Surprise prepares you to learn more about the stimulus that's surprised you, and helps you to plan actions for dealing with that stimulus.

Disgust prepares you to avoid harm or distasteful things.

The positivity of emotions like love and happiness can provide you with a welcome energy boost in other areas of your life.

As you've just learned, emotions can motivate you to take action and adapt to your circumstances.

When trying to understand your own needs and the needs of others, emotions function as a form of information.

Rational information gives you a logical perspective of a person's needs, but emotions provide an alternative, equally valid, form of data.

For example, you need to pass along a customer's criticism to one of your employees, who otherwise performs really well in her job. When she arrives in your office, you notice she's looking unusually.

stressed and flustered. Being in tune with her emotions informs your decision to delay giving her the feedback until a better time, when she's feeling calmer and more receptive.

Now, imagine someone approaches you on a sidewalk and instinctively you have a bad feeling about this person – although there's no rational reason for your reaction. When the person offers to assist you with a heavy bag, you politely decline and then move away.

In this case, you've acted based on an emotional "gut feeling" – otherwise known as intuition.

You might be unable to explain your intuitions, but they don't come from nowhere and shouldn't necessarily be ignored. They may come from what you've learned through past experiences or from your subconscious recognition of what's at play in a particular situation.

Emotions also have the power to build relationships. Being aware of your own emotions and how they affect you can make it easier to read other people's emotions too. This helps you recognize where they're coming from and what it is they need, providing an opportunity to connect with others to build strong relationships.

Although emotions can have many positive functions, they can also be destructive. If you don't recognize and manage your emotions properly, they can motivate you to take actions that will harm you in the long run.

Expressing or acting on your emotions in inappropriate ways can have serious consequences – but so too can failing to express the emotions you have.

For example, a clerk is continuously frustrated by the way his colleagues are treating him. Instead of addressing the situation, he goes on with his job, forcing himself to contain his feelings. Eventually, all his bottled-up frustration becomes too great and he lashes out irrationally at his manager. This explosion costs the clerk his job and seriously harms his future employment prospects.

Unfocused, suppressed, or unrecognized emotions can interfere with your natural brain chemistry, which can cause various physical side effects, including impaired concentration, fatigue, and health problems.

Emotions can also cloud your understanding of yourself and others, and so prevent you from acting rationally or building strong relationships.

Question

Which statements accurately depict the power of emotions?

Options:

1. Strong negative emotions can have adverse physical and psychological effects
2. Emotions enable you to make the most logical choices on decisions you face each day
3. Emotions can prompt you to take action to change an unpleasant situation
4. Emotions enable you to perceive things as they really are, based on the facts at hand
5. Sharing intense emotional experiences connects you to others and helps you to develop strong relationships
6. Emotions help you empathize with the needs of others, enabling you to make effective decisions

Answer:

Option 1: This is a correct option. Physical illness and stress can ensue when a person does not recognize and manage negative emotions properly.

Option 2: This is an incorrect option. Emotions can sometimes cloud the decision–making process, preventing you from seeing the most logical choice.

Option 3: This option is correct. Negative emotions can motivate you to take the necessary actions to steer yourself away from unpleasant circumstances.

Option 4: This option is incorrect. Emotions can influence your perspective, sometimes causing you to overlook facts.

Option 5: This is a correct option. When you share emotional experiences with others, you're better able to relate to them. This can lead to the strengthening of existing relationships or development of new ones.

Option 6: This option is correct. When you recognize others' emotions, you're better able to understand their situations, and can take actions that fulfill their needs.

THE ROLE OF EMOTIONS

The role of emotions

You may not realize it, but your emotional state – or mood – affects virtually everything you do. Some of the affected areas include your decisions and actions, your interactions with others, and your performance, at work or elsewhere.

Tom, the manager of a computer store, is a huge baseball fan. One night, Tom's favorite team wins the first game of the season in a particularly dramatic fashion. The next morning, Tom comes to work feeling especially happy.

Follow along as Sonya, the store's bookkeeper, speaks to Tom.

Sonya: Great game last night, wasn't it? *Sonya asks.*

Tom: Yeah, it certainly was. I thought we were sunk, for sure, but Lopez scored those back-to-back home runs out of nowhere. He was awesome! *Tom enthuses.*

Sonya: He's definitely one of my all-time favorites. *Sonya says.*

Sonya: Anyway, I wanted to ask – could I have an hour extra for lunch today? I need to run some errands and it's more convenient to deal with them today, rather than on the weekend. *Sonya is hopeful.*

Tom: Well, the store is really busy at that time...but OK, I guess that's all right. Take the extra time, but just make sure you're back by 3:00 p.m. *Tom says.*

Question

Why do you think Tom may have decided to grant Sonya an extra hour for lunchtime?

Options:

1. It was a purely rational decision because the store would be quiet in the time she wanted to be away

2. He was in a good mood because of his favorite team's victory the previous night

3. Sonya couldn't run her errands at any other time

Answer:

Option 1: This is an incorrect option. The store gets busy at the time Sonya wanted to be away, so Tom's decision wasn't purely rational.

Option 2: This is the correct option. Although the store would be busy and Sonya could have run her errands on the weekend, Tom's good mood probably helped him to consent to her request.

Option 3: This option is incorrect. Sonya could run the errands on the weekend. Using an extra hour during the work day was just more convenient for her.

Occasionally, strong emotions can override rational logic – either in a positive or negative direction. In Sonya's case, Tom would ordinarily have refused because the store gets very busy in the time when she wants to run her errands.

However, Tom was in such a good mood that he made the opposite choice.

Now consider Curtis, who's in a hurry to get to work, but ends up in the slow traffic lane. He's shocked when the driver behind him crashes into the back of his vehicle. Curtis stops, gets out to assess the damage, and wants to confront the driver who rear-ended him. However, the other driver quickly switches lanes and drives away before Curtis can take down the license plate number.

Although the damage isn't too bad, Curtis is outraged at the incident and arrives at his workplace angry.

As the morning progresses, Curtis gets into a few arguments with colleagues, but he puts this down to wrongdoing on their part. Curtis's colleagues, however, see things differently.

Later that day, Curtis finds many colleagues behaving awkwardly in his presence. Eventually, he ask someone what's going on. She says he's been extremely hostile and agitated the whole day. Everyone is avoiding him because they don't want to be on the receiving end of his anger.

In this case, Curtis experienced a powerful emotional reaction – anger – at the beginning of the day. Hours after the accident, the emotion was still with him, causing him to be hostile toward his colleagues.

Physiologically, Curtis remained angry because anger generates a state of nervous-system arousal that persists for a long period. An angry person is more prone to respond in anger to the next irritating stimulus that comes along. So anger builds on anger.

Question

Now think of a time when you had to work on a task that you found incredibly boring.

How would you rate your performance on that task?
Options:
1. Great
2. Average
3. Poor

Answer:
Option 1: Very few people are able to maintain excellent standards in the face of an uninspiring task. You should consider yourself fortunate if, when working on a tremendously boring task, you're able to work as quickly – or to the same high quality – as you would on other tasks.

Option 2: You aren't alone. When faced with a task they find boring, people who usually perform well can find themselves performing at less than their best. For example, their quality of work may drop or they may work more slowly than they would on more interesting tasks.

Option 3: When faced with an uninspiring task, many people perform poorly. They may work extremely slowly – wasting a lot of time on distractions. Or they might turn in inferior quality work. Sometimes they may even fail to complete the work.

When you work on tasks that are exciting and challenging, your performance is generally better than when you face tasks that leave you feeling uninspired or bored.

Even if you don't realize it, emotions like joy, anger, and boredom play a powerful role. They can affect the way you perceive and react to the world and the decisions you make.

Whether your emotions arise at home or at work, they can affect you deeply – both outwardly and inwardly – and for longer periods than you may realize.

As a result, it's vital to be aware of and in tune with your emotions. This helps you to understand where your reactions are coming from, so you can address the real roots of any issues.

This emotional awareness can be referred to as your emotional intelligence quotient – commonly known as EQ – and it can help you to function better and live a more fulfilling and happy life.

Question

One of your colleagues thinks the concept of "emotional awareness" is psychological nonsense that has no real impact on a person's daily life.

Which examples illustrate how being aware of emotions can help him appreciate the role they play in daily life situations?

Options:

1. "You'll never get anywhere if you operate without any emotion."

2. "Did you notice how our team performs so much better when we're all in a good mood?"

3. "When Rafael embarrassed you in front of the whole office, it couldn't have been easy for you to work with him afterwards, could it?"

4. "It just isn't possible to make decisions without emotion."

5. "When Lucy turned down your legitimate request for a raise, do you think her decision could have been affected by her still being mad at you for messing up the Watermark account?"

Answer:

Option 1: This is an incorrect option. This statement is speculative and could be debated. While it's true a lack of emotional awareness is likely to be a handicap in any environment, it's not necessarily true that emotion informs the best business decisions.

Option 2: This option is correct. This statement illustrates the impact emotions can have on work performance.

Option 3: This is a correct option. This statement illustrates how emotions can have an impact on your interactions with other people. No doubt this work relationship was probably quite fragile for some time after this incident.

Option 4: This option is incorrect. It's possible, at least in specific cases, to make purely neutral, rational decisions based on intellect rather than emotion.

Option 5: This option is correct. Emotions can have an impact on the decisions that people make. When emotions are strong, they can even override logic.

Emotions play a crucial role in your everyday life. Among other functions, they can motivate you to take necessary action, help you understand your own needs and the needs of others, and help you connect with other people and build strong relationships.

Your emotions can affect virtually every aspect of your life, including the decisions you make, your interactions with others, and your performance, at work or elsewhere. It's crucial to be in tune with your emotions so that you can recognize and manage them properly

TRAITS ASSOCIATED WITH IQ AND EQ

IQ and EQ

Emotional intelligence

Debora is a manager in a large company. Her team members enjoy working with her – she's always willing to listen to their problems, even if she doesn't have a ready solution. She stays calm and focused on the team's goals, even under pressure. And because she's sensitive to how her employees feel and adapts accordingly, she's easy to get along with.

Marion is a manager in the same company. She's respected for her brilliance and technical knowledge. However her team finds her brusque and imperious. She has a habit of acting like a drill sergeant demanding that her team members obey orders quickly, and she's prone to losing her temper. The result is, when given a choice, most team members prefer working with Debora to working with Marion.

Intelligence is the capacity to reason about information. In the case of emotional intelligence, it's the capacity to reason about emotions and to use the information they provide.

The reason most employees prefer interacting with Debora is that she displays high emotional awareness. Marion may have a higher IQ, but her emotional intelligence quotient, or EQ, is low and this affects her ability to interact with others.

If you have a high EQ, it means you possess a number of skills and abilities. You maintain an awareness of your own emotions and those of others, manage these emotions effectively, and communicate well. You also maintain positive relationships, can motivate yourself, use your intuition, and demonstrate integrity.

See each skill or ability to learn more about how it contributes to emotional intelligence.

Maintain awareness of emotions

Emotional awareness helps you control your own emotions and pick up on those of the people you interact with. Without emotional awareness, you'll be unaware of how your emotions affect the decisions you make and incapable of regulating their influence on your actions. You'll also be incapable of appreciating their effects on others.

Manage emotions effectively

We've all come across people who can't control their tempers or who act on impulse without first stopping to consider the consequences of their actions. These people don't know how to control their emotions and so instead are controlled by them. Without emotional control, you can't manage stress effectively, think clearly, or communicate effectively. This can negatively affect all areas of your life.

Communicate well

People with high EQs are good communicators because they pick up on the nonverbal signals others communicate and understand the effects emotions can have. This helps them listen effectively and make those they interact with feel understood. This also encourages people to communicate more effectively in return.

Maintain positive relationships

You can't understand the emotions of others unless you understand your own, and how they affect both you and the people around you. Showing people you understand their feelings and needs makes them more likely to cooperate with you and encourages them to deal with you more openly. This is important in building strong relationships, personally and in work environments.

Motivate yourself

If you have a high EQ, you recognize your emotions and can channel them productively. They can motivate you to take action, so you don't rely only on external factors to inspire you. For example, harnessing a desire to be a leader could encourage you to take more responsibility at work or start a volunteer group to help the less fortunate.

Use your intuition

People with high EQs know when to delay judgment and when to go with their gut feelings. In the business world, the role of intuition in decision making is underplayed. But being able to act quickly or decisively, especially when there's not a lot of data to support a decision, often depends on intuition.

Demonstrate integrity

Strong relationships depend on trust and demonstrating integrity is an important way to build that trust. If people know they can trust you, they'll feel free to interact with you openly and honestly. Another aspect of behaving with integrity is recognizing and respecting the feelings and needs of others. This doesn't come easy if you have a low EQ.

Instead of focusing only on logic, people with high EQs integrate information from both the logical and emotional parts of the brain. Put more simply, they succeed in unifying the heart and mind.

Question

Edgar volunteers as a counselor at a center for troubled youths.

What characteristics display evidence of his EQ?

Options:

1. He knows when to talk and when to listen

2. He sometimes loses his cool, but always apologizes

3. He respects the confidentiality of the conversations he has with the youths he works with

4. He enjoys drawing up plans for people to follow

5. He isn't paid for his time, but continues to volunteer it

6. He stays in contact with the youths he works with, even after they leave the center

Answer:

Option 1: This is a correct option. Good communication skills are an important part of high EQ.

Option 2: This option is incorrect. Managing your emotions well is a key part of EQ. Edgar needs to learn to control his emotions, rather than allowing them to control him.

Option 3: This option is correct. Edgar understands that trust and integrity go hand in hand and are important in dealing with others. If the youths trust him, they're more likely to confide in him and he'll be better able to help them.

Option 4: This is an incorrect option. The ability to think rationally and logically is a feature of IQ, not EQ.

Option 5: This option is correct. Edgar is motivated to volunteer because he believes he's doing something important.

Option 6: This is a correct option. Being able to build strong, lasting relationships is a sign of high EQ.

The value of EQ in business

Traditionally, businesses have valued rational, logical thought processes over emotional ones – in other words, IQ over EQ. Increasingly though, research shows that emotional skills are better all-round predictors of people's success.

That's not to say that IQ – or people's intellectual capacity – is unimportant. People with high IQs generally have wide intellectual capacity and a range of interests, confidence and fluency in expressing their opinions, and strong mental abilities – such as those affecting perception, reasoning, and memory. They may also have a greater tendency to worry, which isn't always a negative characteristic.

See each trait to find out more about it.

Wide intellectual capacity and range of interests

People with high IQs tend to be curious about the world around them and to pursue their thirst for knowledge in a range of areas. They have little trouble appreciating a variety of different experiences and areas of knowledge. For example, someone with a high IQ may work as an engineer but compose music or study in another field as a hobby.

Fluency in expressing opinions

High IQ includes verbal intelligence, or the ability to reason about verbal information. So people with high IQs tend to be able to express and substantiate their thoughts and opinions clearly. If they have low EQs, however, they may fail to account for a lack of understanding or a similar ability to substantiate arguments in others.

Strong mental abilities

High IQ generally correlates to high mental abilities in all areas. These include abilities such as being able to note small differences and similarities between objects or ideas, to think quickly of and understand words and their meanings, and to perform mental arithmetic, visualize objects, and apply sets of rules.

Tendency to worry

People with high IQs may be prone to worry more than others because they're used to thinking through possible consequences and outcomes. Worrying can be a productive process because it prompts them to rehearse possible scenarios before they occur, and so can help them find solutions. However, anxiety can also cause them to become trapped in a cycle of negative thoughts, and so cripple their performance.

So IQ is important – people without technical expertise and good intellectual powers of reasoning are unlikely to excel. But IQ isn't everything.

People with high EQs exhibit a range of traits different from those with high IQs, including the ability to maintain a high sense of self-worth and to recognize and understand emotions in themselves and others. And they tend to be easygoing, stay realistic about their abilities, regulate their emotions well, keep themselves motivated, exhibit strong social skills, and express their feelings clearly.

Question

James has a high EQ.

What do you think are the benefits this can have for him in a work environment?

Options:

1. He finds it easy to obtain cooperation from his colleagues 2. He's more likely to be successful at his job

3. He gets better at his job over time

4. He understands the environment he works in

5. He has better ideas than his colleagues

6. He suppresses his emotions to prevent them from interfering with his work

Answer:

James's high EQ means that it's easy for others in a work environment to get along with him. He understands his environment well, and his willingness to improve himself makes him far more likely to achieve success in the workplace.

Option 1: People with high EQ are excellent team players whom others enjoy interacting with. This makes it easy for James to work as part of a team.

Option 2: Nothing can guarantee James success in the workplace, but having a high EQ can significantly increase his chances of achieving it.

Option 3: Having a high EQ enables you to accept and use feedback to develop yourself and improve your skills. James is far more likely to put in the effort to do this than his low-EQ colleagues are.

Option 4: People with high EQs are in touch with their emotions and those of the people around them. Appreciating the impact emotions have on thoughts and actions gives James a greater understanding of his environment.

Option 5: Having a high EQ helps James communicate his ideas more effectively, but it doesn't make his ideas any better than those of his colleagues.

Option 6: Emotional control is central to EQ, but it involves being in touch with and experiencing your emotions, not suppressing them. Instead of wasting energy stifling his emotions, James puts them to work for him.

People who have high EQs are the ones other people want to work with. They remain aware of their emotions and those of the people around them, and treat others in a way that makes them feel valued.

By displaying integrity and character, they inspire trust and openness in all their dealings. As a result, people respond to them well.

This is particularly true in fields like sales, where your success depends heavily on how well you interact with your customers. However, being able to communicate well and work as part of a team is an advantage in almost all jobs.

High EQ can have more personal benefits as well. Keeping yourself open to feedback can clarify areas in which you can improve your performance, in the workplace and outside it.

The emotional awareness and control that comes with a high EQ also gives you a better understanding of the motivations and actions of people around you. This understanding is important in dealing with others and is of great value in work areas like management.

Did the qualities you thought of include things like being a good listener, inspiring and guiding others, displaying vision, and being a good motivator? Note how all these traits are related to EQ, rather than IQ.

They're not functions of general intelligence or technical brilliance, but rather of excellent social skills. Visionaries understand that EQ is what makes a good leader into a great one.

Many businesses have incorporated this knowledge into their hiring processes – to be a successful candidate, you need to possess a high EQ. Fortunately, while IQ is considered to be relatively fixed, you can learn to develop your EQ.

Even if you have a high IQ, a low EQ can handicap you in various ways. It can mean you'll have difficulty building and maintaining strong relationships, decreased ability to motivate yourself, and limited understanding of those around you. Social isolation can be especially harmful to your career – if colleagues don't want to work with you, you have a lower chance of promotion.

Consider the following example. Michael, an experienced engineer, and Scott, a recent doctoral graduate, have applied for the same engineering post. Michael scores higher on his exams than Scott and has more work experience. However, he has a record of letting his temper get the better of him and of not getting along well with his colleagues.

This contrasts starkly with Scott, who's polite and personable. He lacks Michael's onsite experience, but his willingness to learn and easy-going nature make him a natural team player. His designs are less sophisticated than Michael's, but his productivity is better because he can control his emotions – even when things don't go his way. He's the engineering firm's natural choice.

Here's another example. Gail and Erika work in the cosmetics department of a large store. Gail knows the store's entire catalog by heart and is skilled at matching customers' descriptions of what they require with the right products. However, she can be tactless and often inadvertently makes her clients feel insulted. This hurts her sales figures and has led to several customer complaints.

Erika sometimes has to refer to the company's electronic catalog when dealing with customers. They don't mind though, because she makes them feel good about themselves and their purchases. She picks up on their emotions and actual needs – rather than listening only to what they convey verbally – and tailors her responses accordingly. Consequently, she has the highest sales figures in the department.

Both Michael and Gail are intelligent, technically competent people. What has hurt them is their lack of EQ. Michael lacks emotional control and may not even realize how his emotions affect his behavior, or the impact of this on his career. And Gail lacks an awareness of the emotions of others, which compromises her work performance.

Case Study: Question 1 of 2
Scenario

William and Tracy work together. William is known for his technical acumen and for expressing himself clearly and logically. He has a tendency to worry, becomes bogged down when under pressure, and often seems aloof. Tracy is also known for her technical acumen and intelligence. Although she seems reserved initially, colleagues think highly of her and come to her for advice or just to talk problems over. She stays calm under pressure and keeps herself motivated even when things don't appear to be going well.

Answer the questions in order.

Question:

Who is more likely to be successful in the workplace?

Options:

1. William, because he demonstrates a higher IQ
2. William, because he demonstrates a higher EQ
3. Tracy, because she demonstrates a higher IQ
4. Tracy, because she demonstrates a higher EQ

Answer:

Option 1: This option is incorrect. Both employees are known for their technical expertise, so it's hard to say whether William has a higher IQ than Tracy. Also, IQ typically contributes less than a person's EQ to their success in the workplace.

Option 2: This option is incorrect. William has a tendency to let his anxiety control him and is less able to interact positively with the people around him. This is indicative of a lower EQ.

Option 3: This is an incorrect option. Both William and Tracy possess traits typically associated with a high IQ and it's hard to say who's IQ is higher. However, IQ is generally a less effective predictor of success than a person's EQ.

Option 4: This is the correct option. Tracy appears to have a higher EQ than William. She's able to build and maintain strong relationships, control her emotions, and remain calm and motivated. This is likely to make it easier for her to succeed in the workplace.

Case Study: Question 2 of 2

Which of Tracy's traits demonstrate a high EQ?

Options:

1. She builds strong relationships with people around her
2. She stays calm under pressure
3. She keeps herself motivated
4. She's smart and talented
5. She displays great technical expertise

Answer:

Option 1: This option is correct. Building and maintaining strong relationships with others demonstrates a high EQ. It shows Tracy can deal with people in a way that respects their emotions and controls her own emotions.

Option 2: This is a correct option. Emotional self-control is a sign of a high EQ. In this case, it enables Tracy to remain calm under pressure.

Option 3: This option is correct. Self-motivation is associated with a high EQ. It involves channeling emotions productively so they inspire positive action.

Option 4: This option is incorrect. Being smart or talented is a sign of IQ, rather than EQ. While valuable in the workplace, these traits don't relate to emotional awareness or control.

Option 5: This is an incorrect option. This trait is associated with a high IQ rather than a high EQ.

Your emotional intelligence quotient, or EQ for short, is important to your success in life. It covers a variety of skills, including maintaining awareness of and managing emotions, communicating well, motivating yourself, and using your intuition.

EQ is now seen as more important than IQ in work contexts. Traits associated with high IQ include a wide range of interests, strong mental abilities, and a tendency to worry. Traits associated with high EQ include high self-worth, being easygoing, an ability to express feelings clearly, and good social skills.

IMPROVING EMOTIONAL INTELLIGENCE

Improving emotional intelligence

Emotional intelligence competency areas

Rick is a writer for a popular magazine. He's good at his job and highly productive. However, Rick's editor complains he doesn't mix well with his colleagues. He has a reputation for being short-tempered and just doesn't "click" with other people. This, says the editor, is the reason Rick isn't advancing in the company.

Rick has trouble controlling his emotions and relating effectively to others. So even if he's highly intelligent in other areas, it's likely he has a low emotional intelligence quotient – or a low EQ.

What is it that makes it harder for some than for others to manage their emotions and to fit in socially?

The body of knowledge surrounding EQ has grown substantially over recent years. American psychologist Daniel Goleman is responsible for much of the early work on this subject, but others have joined in expanding and refining his work.

With growing understanding of EQ, it's possible to identify the specific sets of skills – or competencies – that make one person more adept at interpreting and managing emotions than another.

A basic model of emotional intelligence consists of four key competency areas – self-awareness, self-management, empathy, and relationship management.

See each competency area for a description of what it involves.

Self-awareness

Self-awareness involves recognizing your emotions, their causes, and their impact on your thoughts, actions, and communications with others. Many people consider self-awareness to be the most important aspect of emotional intelligence.

Self-management

Self-management involves controlling or regulating your own emotions, rather than acting on them instinctively.

Empathy

Empathy encompasses awareness and understanding of the emotions of others.

Relationship management

Relationship management refers to management over the way you interact with others, which determines your ability to establish and maintain strong relationships.

One way of illustrating the dimensions of emotional intelligence and how each of the four competencies relate to these is to use a two-by-two matrix. In the matrix, each competency is either personal or social, and focused either on emotional awareness or management.

In a two-by-two matrix, the two rows are labeled Personal and Social and the two columns are labeled Awareness and Management.

Each cell in the matrix contains one of the four competency areas. Self-awareness is personal and relates to awareness. Self-management is also personal but relates to management. Empathy is social and relates to awareness, and relationship management is social and relates to management.

Each of the competency areas is related. For example, if you struggle to identify or manage your own emotions, it's likely you'll also find it hard to empathize with others and to build strong relationships.

However, each competency area is discrete in that it's associated with specific skills and abilities.

An example of a skill associated with self-awareness is the ability to observe your own emotional reactions by experiencing and understanding them. So if stress is a problem for you, knowing the symptoms and recognizing what you're feeling as stress is the first step to being able to then take action to control it.

Once you're aware of your emotions, you're in a position to manage them appropriately. This leads to the self-management competency area. Self-management deals with regulating your emotions. This is what enables you to remain in control. It prevents you from behaving impulsively, carelessly, or without regard for the likely consequences.

For example, once you realize you're under stress, you might use a mental technique like a quick breathing exercise – or a more physical approach like going for a brisk walk – to reduce your stress.

Failing to control your emotions and then instinctively acting out on them can have disastrous consequences, especially in social settings.

People use a variety of skills to manage their emotions. For example, they step back from what they're feeling and think before they act. They know how to stay focused on getting a job done, rather than allowing themselves to overreact to minor problems. They may also use strategies like humor to defuse strong emotions and put their feelings in perspective.

As well as general self-control, personal qualities that help people manage their emotions include ambition, flexibility, and optimism.

See each quality for more information about how it relates to emotional self-management.

Ambition

Ambition can help you focus on achieving your goals, rather than allowing your emotional reactions to distract you from this.

Flexibility

Being flexible helps ensure you're comfortable adapting to new circumstances, including when things go wrong. It involves being able to let go of what you're feeling and to move on.

Optimism

Optimism can help you overcome more negative emotions or regulate them by putting them in a broader, more positive context.

Whereas self-awareness and self-management are personal competencies, empathy is a social one. It's what enables you to recognize and understand the feelings, needs, and wants of other people, even if they're not openly expressed.

These are some of the other qualities that make you empathetic:
- be a good listener, actively listening to others and picking up on their emotions and perspectives,
- recognize and meet the needs of others, and
- understand decision-making styles and politics at an organizational level, based on the emotional needs or motivations of those involved.

The final competency area, associated with your social skills, is relationship management. If you are able to manage your relationships, you're likely to communicate well with others and build strong relationships.

This, in turn, can boost productivity and lead to enhancements in several other abilities, including leadership, influence, mentorship, and teamwork.

See each ability to learn how good relationship management can enhance it.

Leadership

Being a good leader involves being able to earn trust and to inspire, motivate, and guide others. So it depends heavily on how well you interact with other people.

Influence

If you have strong relationships and communicate easily, you'll automatically gain greater influence over others. They'll be more likely to relate to and support your arguments.

Mentorship

Good relationship management enables you to mentor others, because they trust you to guide and help them in their tasks. This, in turn, helps them to develop.

Teamwork

If you're good at maintaining healthy relationships, you'll be better equipped to cooperate and collaborate with other members of a team.

Some theorists also suggest that motivation is an element of EQ, noting that emotionally intelligent individuals are usually driven to succeed, up for challenges, and very productive.

Question

Match examples of skills and abilities to the corresponding competency areas. More than one example may match to an area.

Options:

A. The ability to understand your own feelings

B. The ability to know how organizational-level politics affect an individual's behavior

C. The ability to not act out disruptive emotions

D. The ability to relate to others and motivate and guide a team

E. The ability to recognize when emotions affect outcomes

F. The ability to adjust to unexpected obstacles

Targets:

1. Self-awareness
2. Empathy
3. Self-management
4. Relationship management

Answer:

Self-awareness encompasses the ability to recognize your own feelings and their causes. It's also associated with being aware of the effect a specific emotion may have on a specific event, so you can then leverage other EQ competencies to deal with it.

Empathy is associated with the ability to recognize and understand the feelings, needs, and wants of other people – even if they're not openly expressed, which is often the case in organizational–level politics.

Self-management encompasses the ability to regulate emotions, which involves such things as keeping disruptive emotions under control and adjusting to unexpected obstacles.

Relationship management encompasses the social skills involved in relating well to others. These can, for instance, improve your ability to motivate and guide a team.

Assessment and development

Emotional intelligence isn't innate. You aren't born with it. It's something you develop and learn through life experiences. So it's possible to improve on your skills in each of the four associated competency areas.

You can begin this process by assessing your EQ. The result of this assessment will help you identify competency areas in which you're weak.

You can perform an assessment in a number of ways. This is an example of an EQ self-assessment tool consisting of a number of statements, each of which represents one or more competency areas. To use the tool, you rate yourself on each statement and then tally up the results to find out where your weaknesses lie.

Question

Match the statements from the example tool to the competency areas they assess. Some competency areas may match to more than one statement.

Options:

A. I relate well to others and can build relationships with people from all walks of life

B. I'm mindful of the way my behavior affects others

C. I focus on finishing the task at hand – I don't get distracted by my emotions

D. I'm able to recognize when my frustration is starting to turn to resentment

E. I'm good at looking at situations from someone else's perspective

Targets:

1. Relationship management
2. Self-awareness
3. Self-management
4. Empathy

Answer:

Relationship management skills and abilities are characterized by our ability to manage our relationships with others – such as our colleagues, clients, and managers – both by being able to communicate well and using this ability to build relationships.

Self-awareness is characterized by the ability to be in tune with what our behavior or emotions are at any given time, and how this affects situations. Self-awareness is the key to other competency areas as well. For example, before you can build relationships, you need to be aware of how your behavior affects others.

Self-management is characterized by our ability to regulate or manage our own emotions so they don't distract us from the situation or cause disruptions. Self-managment enables us to stop ourselves from reacting impulsively based on immediate emotional responses.

Empathy is characterized by our ability to put ourselves in someone else's shoes and see how they might feel about a situation.

Once you've identified your weak areas, you can develop an action plan to address them. Your action plan might include all four competency areas or it may focus on particular areas of weakness.

To develop your self-awareness, you should consciously observe your own emotional reactions. Allow yourself to experience these reactions, and try to understand why you're reacting in a certain way. For example, if you dislike someone you just met, is your reaction based on a stereotype you have about this person?

Another strategy is to observe your triggers. What events or interactions trigger specific emotional reactions? For example, if someone regularly fails to acknowledge your efforts, you may feel resentment each time you're not acknowledged.

One way to apply the strategies for improving self-awareness is to take some time at the end of each day to review any incidents that evoked strong emotions in you. Recall each event and document what happened, how it made you feel, and how you reacted. You can also dig deeper, trying to find if there's an underlying source of a particular emotion – such as an unpleasant experience in your past.

Once you've identified your emotions, you can move onto assessing how well you managed these. Were your reactions appropriate? If they were unwarranted or too extreme, you can try to make changes that will help you react in a more balanced way in the future. In particular, important strategies in self-management are to think before you act and to manage your triggers.

See each strategy to find out more about it.

Think before you act

Once you realize you're experiencing a destructive or particularly strong emotion, step back from the situation and take some time to think. You should pause to consider the best way to react, rather than reacting immediately on impulse.

Manage your triggers

When you know what your negative triggers are, you can anticipate your immediate emotional reactions to those situations. It's a good idea to take the time to assess your triggers and then plan better ways of reacting to them. That way, when you spot one of your triggers on the horizon, you can respond with a planned reaction, rather than with one that's instinctive and potentially inappropriate.

Applying self-management strategies to issues you've identified as part of your self-awareness evaluation can help develop both of these competencies.

For example, recognizing how an incident made you feel, gives you an opportunity to think about how you could reframe that feeling before you take action next time.

Finally, you can identify a more appropriate action to take the next time the reaction is triggered.

To enhance your empathy, you need to recognize that other people's experiences may lead them to react to situations in different ways. Before judging or reacting to someone, consider the other person's perspective. Put yourself in their shoes by asking questions such as these – How do they feel about the situation? What do they want? What do they need? and Would I like to be in their position?

By stepping out of your own mental space and into someone else's, you're more likely to understand their feelings and needs. In turn, this will enable you to be more open and accepting of the other person.

To improve your relationship management skills, you should consider your actions carefully, acknowledge the emotions of others, and take responsibility for your actions.

See each strategy to find out more about it.

Consider your actions carefully

Before saying or doing something, consider how your actions will affect others. If your action will harm your relationship with another person unnecessarily, you can change your plans accordingly.

Acknowledge others

You can acknowledge another person's emotions in several ways, either openly or more subtly.

For example, if a colleague is feeling down, you can lift his spirits by telling him of something he did to make you feel good. Or if a colleague is frustrated by a lack of opportunities to impress management, step aside and let her take over one of your responsibilities.

Take responsibility

If you wrong someone, take responsibility for your action and apologize directly to this person. Avoiding the person or ignoring the incident can make the situation worse, whereas being honest and acknowledging your mistake can help you repair your relationship.

Improving your emotional intelligence skills can be a long and difficult journey. It requires brutal honesty and admission to your weaknesses. If you've avoided those weaknesses for years or even decades, this can be difficult.

But by embarking on this process with courage and commitment, you can improve areas of your emotional intelligence. In turn, this can help you to live a better, more fulfilling life.

Question

Match each EQ competency area with the strategy or strategies you can use to strengthen your skills and abilities in that area.

Some competency areas may match to more than one strategy.

Options:

A. Self-awareness

B. Empathy

C. Self-management

D. Relationship Management

Targets:

1. Reflect on your reactions to situations and identify the emotions behind the reactions

2. Put yourself in the other person's shoes to understand what might have caused them to react in a certain way

3. Anticipate your negative triggers and have a plan in place for handling them

4. Examine how your actions have affected others and take responsibility for those actions

5. Acknowledge the feelings and emotions of others

6. Recognize that other people's experiences shape their emotional reactions

Answer:

The self-awareness competency area is almost like the gateway to all other competency areas. You need to understand your own emotions before you can begin to use that knowledge to develop the other areas. Taking the time to reflect on your reactions to the events in your life and the emotions behind those reactions can open the floodgates of understanding needed to develop the other competencies.

To develop the empathy competency area, it's important to be able to perceive things as others do. This helps you understand why they act or react the way they do to you or to situations.

Self-management involves recognizing and then managing your triggers so you don't act impulsively on your emotions.

Taking responsibility when you've wronged someone is an important strategy to develop the relationship management competency area. An apology or acknowledgement of a misstep reassures others you're invested in the relationship and that you're only human.

One way to develop the relationship management competency area is to acknowledge the feelings and emotions of others. This lets them know you care, which is the foundation of strong relationships.

Knowing you're shaped by your own experiences is an important understanding that will strengthen your empathy competency area.

The emotional intelligence quotient – or a person's EQ – is made up of four key competency areas. These include self-awareness, self-management, empathy, and relationship management.

You can improve your skills in each competency area using a variety of techniques. A useful first step is identifying your weaknesses and developing a plan specifically to address these.

CHAPTER II - SELF-AWARENESS AND SELF-MANAGEMENT

CHAPTER II - Self-awareness and Self-management

In this book, you'll learn various strategies for improving your self-awareness and self-management skills:
- the value of being self-aware, how to recognize different emotions, and techniques for developing your self-awareness,
- the value of self-management and the ability to control your emotional reactions, and
- various self-management techniques and how to apply them in your own life.
-

THE VALUE OF EMOTIONAL SELF-AWARENESS

The value of emotional self-awareness

Becoming self-aware is the first step in acquiring emotional intelligence. You have to be aware of your emotions before you can manage them.

Every day at work, Mark, who's known as a highly competent accountant, has an uncomfortably tight feeling in his stomach and chest. His palms are always sweaty and he has occasional outbursts that he can't explain. One day, he stands up in the middle of an important meeting, shouts "I've had enough of this", and marches out.

Later, Mark has trouble explaining his behavior. He's always focusing on his work and hasn't ever stopped to consider what he's actually feeling or why.

The problem is that ignoring your emotions, or pretending they don't exist, doesn't simply make them go away.

Self-awareness is the first of four essential competencies that make up your emotional intelligence.

Self-awareness is the foundation on which all the other competencies build. For example, you can't manage your emotions if you don't recognize them, and you can't empathize with others if you're not familiar with emotions and their effects. And if you can't control your emotions or read them in others, you'll struggle to build strong relationships.

Being emotionally self-aware goes beyond just realizing, for example, that you're happy, upset, or anxious. It involves recognizing and understanding your own emotions, their causes, and their effects on your thoughts and behavior.

People who are self-aware are willing and able to take an honest look at themselves. They're constantly aware of their moods, why they have those moods, and how these affect their performance and interactions with others.

Many different components determine the state of your self-awareness, including your emotions, your physical actions, your preferences and intentions, your goals and values, and your knowledge of how other people see you.

Were you able to pinpoint your emotions and their causes? This is a starting point for being self-aware. It's important to be aware of your feelings for several reasons:

- it enables you to understand how emotions affect your behavior,
- recognizing your feelings enables you to experience them fully so you can learn from and enjoy your emotions, and
- self-awareness enables you to choose whether to express your emotions and how.

See each benefit of emotional self-awareness for more information.

Understand how emotions affect behavior

Emotions – including ones you don't recognize – affect your behavior. If you're unaware of what you're feeling or why, your emotions can cloud your judgment and lead you to behave inappropriately.

For example, anger can prevent you from perceiving a situation – even one that didn't prompt your anger – clearly. It may cause you to overlook facts and make rash decisions you'll regret later. Similarly, if you're frustrated or annoyed about something else, you might snap or yell at the next person who simply asks something of you.

If you recognize your emotions and the ways they affect your behavior, you can take steps to control them and to ensure your reactions are appropriate.

Learn from your emotions

It's only by recognizing your emotions that you let yourself experience them fully, and this can enrich your life.

Also, recognizing your emotions and observing how they affect you enables you to learn from them. For example, accepting disappointments can help prepare you for other losses in life. Recognizing that frustration, anxiety, and anger affect you in particular ways can also teach you how best to manage these types of emotions in different situations.

Choose how to express emotions

Being aware of your emotions is the first step in making your reactions to them a conscious process. Instead of reacting impulsively or in ways that are potentially inappropriate, you can then choose when and how best to express your feelings. Also, you have to be able to recognize your emotions to express them clearly to others.

You attain emotional self-awareness and progress naturally into self-management by following four steps. First you tune in to your emotions to identify what you're feeling. Next you need to recognize the cause of your emotions and their impact on you. As the third step, you should accept your emotions. And finally, you can take action to manage them appropriately.

Question

Self-awareness is considered by many to be the most important or fundamental component of emotional intelligence.

Why is this?

Options:

1. Being aware of your emotions makes it more likely you'll be able to think clearly before you act 2. Self-awareness enables you to learn from your emotions – both the positive and the negative

3. Understanding your emotions is the first step in managing them so that you can interact well with others

4. Recognizing disruptive emotions is the first step in being able to suppress them so you don't have to deal with them

5. Self-awareness helps shield you from strong emotions, which can cause you to act irrationally

Answer:

Option 1: This option is correct. Self-awareness involves recognizing your emotions, their causes, and their effects on your thoughts and behavior. Doing this helps prevent your feelings from clouding your judgment or making you behave irrationally.

Option 2: This is a correct option. Before you can enjoy your emotions or learn from them, you have to be willing to recognize and experience them.

Option 3: This option is correct. Before you can control your emotions and your reactions to them, you have to recognize them. This is also the first step in being able to recognize and empathize with the feelings of others.

Option 4: This is an incorrect option. The purpose of becoming more emotionally aware is to help you control and deal with your emotions, rather than ignoring or suppressing them.

Option 5: This option is incorrect. Being aware of your feelings and their causes isn't going to protect you from experiencing strong emotions, like anger or grief.

Observing yourself

When's the last time you really examined your emotions or how they influence your behavior? Sometimes doing this truthfully can be frightening or even painful. But improving your self-awareness takes a real commitment – one that's likely to pay off by enriching your personal life and performance at work. Even setting aside a little time each day to cultivate your self-awareness, perhaps when you're driving to work or during a lunch break, can make a significant difference. Four specific techniques can help you improve your self-awareness:

- observing yourself, examining your feelings and how they affect you,
- getting to know yourself and what triggers specific emotions in you,

- developing and using your emotional vocabulary, and
- asking others for feedback about your emotional responses so that you can learn from it.

The first technique, observing yourself, involves mentally detaching from your emotions and examining them – as well as how they affect you – like a neutral third party. Mentally watching yourself and your behavior in this way can help you become more aware of your emotions and your responses to them.

When observing yourself, you can ask various questions:
- How do I feel right now?
- What triggered this emotion, or caused it in me?
- Is this feeling serving me well now or is it actually harmful?
- What is affecting decisions I make?
- How do I feel about my decisions?

When you're observing yourself, you may do so in the present. Or you may picture your experiences and behavior in the past – or even envision future situations and picture your likely reactions.

See each timeframe for more information about how you can observe yourself as a strategy for becoming more self-aware.

Present

Observing yourself in the present can be very useful. Examine your emotions, and then stop and think what you're really feeling, why, and how you're being affected.

If you feel irritated, for example, recognize this and ask yourself why. Also ask yourself what physical reactions you're having because of what you're feeling and how this is affecting your behavior – including your interactions with people around you.

Past

You can go back in time and review situations in which you experienced strong emotions to examine exactly what you felt and how it affected your thoughts and behavior.

For example, you snapped at someone at work. What were you really feeling at the time, and why?

Future

To observe yourself in future situations, you can construct hypothetical situations in which you're likely to experience particular emotions.

For example, if your manager criticizes you during a performance appraisal despite the long hours you've been putting into your job, how are you likely to feel? And how is this feeling likely to affect your actions?

When you're observing your emotional responses in different situations, it's helpful to study your physical reactions. These can help you recognize what it is you're feeling. For example, you should focus on the feelings or positions of your neck, shoulders, jaw, throat, forehead, abdomen, and chest.

Also consider your heart rate, breathing, perspiration, and muscle tightness.

People experience a host of different emotions, including positive ones like joy and relief. However, three emotions that can be particularly pervasive in their impact are anger, sadness or grief, and excessive worry. Each of these is associated with particular physical responses.

See each type of emotion for more information about the associated physical and behavioral responses.

Anger

Physical signs of anger include clenching your jaw, increased heart rate, sweating and feeling hot, and breathing more rapidly. Behaviorally, anger can make you pace, repeat a thought or phrase in your head, raise your voice, and become abrasive or sarcastic.

Anger is one of the most difficult emotions to control because it often builds – it predisposes you to become angrier still in response to minor irritations. In a work environment, it may lead you to behave inappropriately, damaging your relationships with team members, managers, or customers.

Sadness or grief

Symptoms of sadness or grief can include a lack of energy and general fatigue, either oversleeping or insomnia, restlessness, and difficulty concentrating. Sadness can also cause you to draw away from others and dispense with your normal activities, leading to isolation and loneliness.

Everyone experiences sadness or grief at some point, when they lose someone or something important to them. However, it's important to deal with this emotion and not to be overcome by it.

Excessive worry

Worrying can actually be healthy – it can help you prepare mentally for problems that might arise. However, excessive worry can impair your performance and ability to be rational.

Signs that you're worrying excessively include shortness of breath, tense muscles, a fluttering feeling in the chest or stomach, sweaty palms, and a dry mouth. Behaviorally, you may appear overly apprehensive or timid, withdraw from others, and become unable to focus on anything other than the source of your worry. This can make you difficult to be around and compromise your ability to function properly in a team.

Question

Match each emotion to an example of its physical and behavioral manifestation. An emotion may match to more than one example.

Options:

A. Anger
B. Excessive worry
C. Sadness or grief

Targets:

1. In a meeting, you feel hot, clench your jaw, and repeat the last thing a colleague said over and over again in your mind
2. You experience shortness of breath, catastrophic thinking, and a fluttering feeling in your chest
3. You find you're not interested in socializing, having trouble concentrating, and constantly feeling tired
4. When you get to work you have a really dry mouth and sweaty palms
5. After your manager asks you to amend a report, you pace, your heart beats faster, and you make a sarcastic remark

Answer:

Repeating a phrase in your head, feeling hot, and clenching your jaw are all physical and behavioral manifestations of anger.

Shortness of breath, catastrophic thinking, and a fluttering feeling in your chest or stomach are all physical and behavioral manifestations of excessive worry.

Withdrawing from people, lack of energy, and difficulty concentrating are all physical and behavioral manifestations of sadness or grief.

A dry mouth and sweaty palms are both physical manifestations of excessive worry.

Sarcastic behavior, getting louder, and pacing are all physical and behavioral manifestations of anger.

TECHNIQUES FOR BUILDING SELF-AWARENESS

Techniques for building self-awareness

Getting to know yourself

Have you ever made a decision or behaved in a certain way and then wondered why you did? The second technique for becoming more emotionally self-aware is simply getting to know yourself properly – essentially, to understand what makes you tick.

To get to know yourself better, you should ask yourself questions. For example, what's important to you and what do your activities tell you about your passions and preferences? This will help you understand your goals and values.

Knowing yourself is essential for identifying what makes you feel the way you do in various situations. This is an essential aspect of self-awareness.

Developing an emotional vocabulary

To help you pinpoint how you're feeling, it's useful to develop and use your emotional vocabulary.

Emotions don't just come in a few standard varieties – they are nuanced and complex, and true self-awareness requires that you recognize the different shades of emotion.

For example, describing yourself just as feeling "sad" can mean a range of things. You could be feeling slightly down, dissatisfied, or completely devastated. By using the correct vocabulary to describe your mood to yourself, you clarify what it is you're feeling.

Asking for feedback

A final technique for improving your self-awareness is to ask for feedback about your emotional responses from trusted colleagues or friends. People who know you well may be able to help you recognize patterns in your behavior, as well as letting you know how you come across to others.

For example, Margaret asks her close colleague, Phil, if he notices anything about her behavior at work. Phil has noticed a few things, and points out that Margaret becomes very apprehensive and tends to develop tunnel vision when she has a deadline or is running late.

Margaret's behavior indicates she's prone to excessive worry. This may make it difficult for her to concentrate, which can have a negative effect on her work. By asking for feedback, Margaret has identified an area that she can work on to improve.

A further strategy you can use when applying the techniques for improving your self-awareness is to set a reminder to "check in" with your emotions. This can prompt you to examine your feelings and their causes, and to ask for feedback from others.

It can also be helpful to record your impressions. This won't always be feasible, but it can be very helpful to refer back to a record of your impressions when processing information about your emotions.

When you're working on improving your emotional self-awareness, it's inevitable that you'll discover some bad with the good. For example, you may discover things you don't like about yourself. Remember though, it's important to accept that you always have room to improve – and weaknesses can represent opportunities.

Question

You have trouble controlling your reactions at work and decide it's time to become more aware about your emotions and how they're affecting your behavior.

What are examples of ways you can do this?

Options:

1. Set aside some time to consider how you felt and reacted in particular situations that triggered emotional responses

2. Consciously ask yourself about your values and goals, and question what makes you respond in certain ways

3. Expand the vocabulary you use to describe your emotions to yourself

4. Ask someone you trust and who knows you well for an opinion on how you tend to respond in emotional situations

5. Ask your new manager if your emotional responses tend to be appropriate

6. Focus on assessing what makes you angry and how you typically respond to this

Answer:

Option 1: This option is correct. Observing yourself – what you feel and how this makes you react, both physically and in terms of your behavior – is an important technique for improving your self-awareness.

Option 2: This is a correct option. Getting to know yourself and what prompts specific emotional reactions in you is a good way to help improve your self-awareness.

Option 3: This is a correct option. Using precise terms to describe emotions can help you pinpoint exactly what you're feeling in different circumstances.

Option 4: This is a correct option. An important step in becoming more self-aware is asking for feedback from others who know you well. This can give you perspective and help you identify areas you need to improve on.

Option 5: This option is incorrect. It's good to ask for feedback, but only from someone you trust and who knows you well.

Option 6: This option is incorrect. Being self-aware involves recognizing all your emotions – not just anger – as well as what triggers them in you and how you typically react.

Emotional self-awareness involves recognizing your feelings, their causes, and their effects on you. This is a foundation for all the other competencies that together make up your emotional intelligence.

An important technique for improving your self-awareness is observing yourself, and recognizing your emotions and your reactions to these in various situations.

Additional techniques include getting to know yourself properly, developing and using a broader vocabulary to describe your emotions accurately, and asking for feedback from others.

SELF-MANAGEMENT FUNCTIONS

Self-management functions

Self-awareness and self-control

Have you ever had to deal with a colleague or manager who was a loose cannon or a drama queen? If you have, you'll know how disruptive and counterproductive such behavior can be. But emotional outbursts don't always indicate an underlying personality disorder. Everyone experiences tough times at some points in their life.

Alan, a project manager, is going through a tricky divorce. He has always prided himself on his ability to separate his personal and professional life, so he doesn't tell anyone at the office. But lately, he's struggling to keep his cool. He's easily annoyed, and often loses his temper when things go wrong.

Clearly, Alan's behavior is affecting both his and his team's ability to do their jobs. Bad moods like Alan's are contagious and can poison relationships in the workplace.

Because Alan is in such a foul mood all the time, members of his team have become afraid to approach him with problems related to the project. Colleagues feel they're walking on eggshells around him and are unable to get on with their work. After a particularly aggressive outburst, one employee even ends up running out of his office in tears.

Losing your self-control and allowing strong emotions to overwhelm you is disruptive. It can impair your ability to meet challenges, end up disturbing others, and make you look unprofessional.

In extreme cases, it can also result in job loss, jeopardize promotions, and damage friendships or professional relationships.

It's important to stay positive, and to remain cool and calm in the workplace. But sometimes this is easier said than done. Being aware of your emotions is only the first step – you also need to know what to do with that knowledge and how to self-manage your emotions. Everyone experiences failures, set-

backs, and losses. How you react to and deal with such experiences helps determine how successful you are, both in your personal and professional life.

Preventing emotional breakdowns

When your emotions bubble up and overwhelm your attempts to suppress them, you may have an emotional breakdown. The result of an emotional breakdown is that you lose control of yourself and react involuntarily. We say someone has "lost it" or "gone overboard" when this happens.

Road rage is a classic example of an emotional breakdown, but more subtle examples can often be witnessed in the workplace:

- leaving the room in a huff, slamming the door on the way out,
- exploding with an angry outburst at someone who doesn't deserve it,
- immediately firing off a rude or aggressive e-mail response,
- falling silent and withdrawing from others,
- using aggressive humor or sarcasm to avoid straightforward conversation,
- avoiding certain people or conversations, and
- acting victimized, becoming despondent, and feeling powerless.

You might often struggle to control your behavior when you feel strongly. Or you might find you're prone to emotional breakdowns in particular situations.

In either case, this may make colleagues try to avoid setting you off. They may feel they have to avoid certain subjects in your presence, or feel they're at fault when you lose control.

So for the sake of both your professional and personal relationships, it's important to stay in control of your emotional reactions.

You might often struggle to control your behavior when you feel strongly. Or you might find you're prone to emotional breakdowns in particular situations.

In either case, this may make colleagues try to avoid setting you off. They may feel they have to avoid certain subjects in your presence, or feel they're at fault when you lose control.

So for the sake of both your professional and personal relationships, it's important to stay in control of your emotional reactions.

Question

What do you think self-control involves?

Options:

1. Allowing yourself to have emotions but controlling your reactions to them
2. Managing your emotions so nobody can tell what you're feeling
3. Suppressing negative emotions and giving positive ones free reign

Answer:

Option 1: This is the correct option. Self-management involves acknowledging your emotions and knowing how to handle them rather than trying to suppress or deny them.

Option 2: This is an incorrect option. While at times you may need to tone it down, it's better to admit your emotions to yourself and others. Self-control involves knowing how to express yourself, not hiding your feelings away.

Option 3: This is an incorrect option. It's impossible to suppress your emotions entirely – they'll find a way to show themselves, usually in the form of an emotional breakdown. Self-managment involves recognizing emotions – both positive and negative – and knowing how to deal with them.

Whereas self-awareness is the foundation of emotional intelligence, self-management is about making the right decisions about what to do with your emotions.

It involves taking action such as expressing your feelings when they're relevant, and dealing with irrelevant or inappropriate emotions – whether they're positive or negative – in the right way.

Letting yourself react instinctively to a positive emotion can be just as inappropriate as acting out a negative one. For example, it would be inappropriate to shout with joy in front of your colleagues if you're the only one given a raise.

Remember that over-control – where you don't share or express your emotions at all – can be just as problematic as a complete lack of control.

Self-control isn't about trying to fake or suppress your emotions. This could negatively affect your health. It may also be counterproductive, because your true feelings could eventually explode in an inappropriate way.

If you bottle up your feelings and try not to show any vulnerability at all, you run the risk of appearing aloof and unfeeling. Your emotions are what make you human and can help you connect to other people.

What probably comes to mind first when you think of self-control is managing to keep your cool in the face of negative emotions like anger. For example, you may use a technique like taking a deep breath or counting to ten to resist the urge to lash out. However, other less intuitive ways can help you demonstrate self-control. These include being assertive, showing resilience, and moderating the tone of conversations.

See each response that demonstrates self-control to find out more about it.

Being assertive

Being assertive generally involves channeling your feelings into getting something productive done, rather than simply reacting instinctively. This demonstrates self-control.

Often being assertive also requires courage – recognizing a fear or avoidance tendency and purposefully overcoming it. For example, it may require courage to voice dissent at a meeting, challenge a coworker who's behavior is inappropriate, or initiate a difficult conversation with your boss.

Showing resilience

Your resilience is your ability to bounce back from difficult situations. If you're resilient, you don't let disappointment or other negative emotions get the better of you – so you persevere rather than giving up. For example, an unpublished writer who refuses to get discouraged by rejection letters from publishers is resilient.

Moderating conversations

You manage your emotions when you moderate the tone of a conversation to prevent it from becoming too strongly charged. You may defuse a potential conflict by adjusting what you say – or how you say it – based on how you gauge the other party is likely to react. Or you may subtly guide a conversation that has gone off-track back in the right direction.

For instance, when a colleague reacts with irritation to your request for information, you resist the urge to snap back. Instead, you demonstrate self-control by apologizing and politely asking when is a more suitable time to request the information.

Anticipating strong emotions

A useful self-management strategy is to prepare in advance how you'll handle strong emotions. That way, you'll have the reassurance of a safety net and won't be caught off guard when a stressful situation occurs.

You can rehearse a positive script for a worrying or enraging situation. Develop a response plan for how you might handle a tough upcoming staff meeting, confronting a problematic colleague, or any other challenge you think has the potential to get out of hand.

It also helps to be aware of the triggers that have the potential to evoke strong emotions in you. These triggers may, for example, relate to the moods of others, hot buttons, criticism, and the physical environment.

See each type of emotional trigger for more information about it.

Moods of others

If you're sensitive to the moods and attitudes of others, try to pinpoint who tends to provoke an emotional response in you and why. You could rehearse making light-hearted comments to defuse the situation.

Hot buttons

Certain subjects or words – often referred to as hot buttons – might evoke an overblown or irrational emotional reaction from you, because of past experiences or specific beliefs you have. You could imagine laughing at yourself when this happens or prepare a more diplomatic response than a knee-jerk reaction.

Criticism

A common emotional trigger is criticism, especially when you feel it's unfair or you haven't been given a chance to defend yourself. You could rehearse a calm response like, "Why do you feel that way?"

Physical environment

Specific situations or physical environments can be emotional triggers. For example, you might tend to become irritable when your surroundings are crowded, noisy, or cold. You could try envisioning yourself staying calm in these situations.

You'll go a long way to being able to navigate your emotional responses if you acknowledge what triggers them, visualize positive outcomes, and finally, take steps to make these outcomes a reality.

Question

Which statements about self-management as a component of emotional intelligence are correct?

Options:

1. It involves knowing when and how to express all types of emotions
2. It relies on self-awareness
3. It involves managing your own feelings
4. It has a strong impact on those around you
5. It involves ensuring you don't experience inappropriate emotions
6. It involves suppressing negative emotions and expressing positive ones

Answer:

Option 1: This is a correct option. As a component of emotional intelligence, self-management involves making conscious decisions about how to react appropriately to your emotions, whether they're positive or negative.

Option 2: This option is correct. To control your emotions, you first need to recognize them and their causes.

Option 3: This option is correct. Self-management involves regulating your own feelings and making conscious decisions about how it's appropriate to react to them.

Option 4: This is a correct option. If you're able to regulate your emotions and avoid emotional breakdowns, others will find it easier to get along with you.

Option 5: This option is incorrect. Good self-management involves controlling your emotional reactions, rather than preventing or suppressing them.

Option 6: This is an incorrect option. Having self-control means managing – rather than suppressing – both positive and negative emotions.

Emotional intelligence begins with self-awareness, which involves recognizing your emotions and their causes. The next step is self-management – regulating your emotions and making conscious decisions about how to react to them appropriately.

Self-management prevents emotional breakdowns, in which you lose control over your behavior. Rather than suppressing emotions, it involves acknowledging and dealing with them.

Identifying triggers and potentially stressful situations, and planning in advance how you'll react to the emotions they cause, is a good way to improve your self-management skills.

MANAGING EMOTIONS

Managing emotions

Self-management techniques

Even if you know what you're feeling and why, how do you control your emotions, and your subsequent behavior? What actions can you take to do this?

Three examples of disruptive emotions are anger, excessive worry, and sadness or grief. While it's important to identify and control the whole range of emotions you experience, these three can be the most difficult to manage.

People use a wide variety of techniques to control and manage emotions like anger, worry, and grief – but they won't all be covered here. You might find that some techniques work better for you than others, depending on your own personality and situation.

You probably already have a few techniques of your own. Most people automatically seek out ways to comfort and soothe themselves. For example, someone feeling depressed or despondent might deliberately seek out others in an attempt to cheer up.

Often, effective techniques for controlling negative emotions center on deliberately behaving in a way you find positive and relaxing.

Ways to counteract negative emotions

A variety of techniques can help defuse difficult emotions like anger, anxiety, and grief.

For example, one way to defuse anger is to challenge the thoughts that spark it. This is most effective when undertaken at early or moderate levels of anger.

Distraction can be useful for combating sadness – TV, movies, or reading can take your mind off depressing thoughts.

You can reduce anxiety by engaging in a physical activity, like walking in a natural setting. Deep breathing and relaxation exercises are also effective for counteracting anger or anxiety.

Some of the self-control techniques you'll learn about in this topic include using positive self-talk, giving yourself a reality check, seeking a change of scenery or task, disclosing your emotions to others, and using humor to defuse negative emotions.

Staying positive

Triggers that set off your emotional reactions don't always come from the external environment. They can also come from your own behavior or thought patterns. For example, you may have a tendency to dwell on problems or to expect the worst whenever something goes wrong.

It's easy to fall into different types or patterns of negative thought, including all-or-nothing thought, a tendency to use "should" statements, or a habit of personalization and blame.

See each type of negative thinking for more information about it.

All-or-nothing

When you fall prey to all-or-nothing thinking, you rate your action or your situation as a complete failure if it isn't completely perfect. For example, if your boss gives you mixed feedback on a report you wrote, you focus only on the criticisms and disregard the praise.

A symptom of this type of thought is using generalizations like "always" and "never." You might respond to the feedback by saying "I always mess up!" or "My boss never has anything good to say about me."

"Should" statements

"Should" statements are backward-looking statements about what might have been. When used properly, you can use "should" statements to motivate yourself to do better next time. But often, people plague themselves with guilt-ridden "should" statements about past events they can't change.

Examples are "I shouldn't have said that" or "I should have known better." Often this sort of thinking goes around in circles and simply leads to frustration.

Personalization and blame

One type of negative thinking involves personalizing failures, blaming yourself for them beyond the point that's constructive or objective. You might tell yourself "It's all my fault that the project failed." Similarly, you might blame others for what has gone wrong.

Often people combine personalization or blame with "should" statements or all-or-nothing thinking. They say things like "James never should have joined this team" or "I always go and ruin everything."

You can challenge negative thoughts by consciously using positive self-talk. Essentially, this involves giving yourself a motivating internal pep talk to break the pattern and stop negative thoughts in their tracks. Instead of being be hard on yourself, use gentle, kind words to make yourself feel better.

If you get trapped into thinking "I always mess up," for example, you could counter this with the thought "I'll do better next time."

Or you could challenge a "should" statement like "I should never have taken this job" with "I'll settle down soon."

You might avoid personalization by thinking "It's a pity the project failed, but I'm sure I can learn from the experience."

Giving yourself a reality check

A similar strategy to using positive self-talk is to give yourself a reality check. You do this by deliberately stepping away from your initial emotional impulses and viewing your situation with a different, more objective perspective.

You can use different methods to give yourself a reality check when you're experiencing a difficult emotion. To combat anger, you can reframe the situation. Excessive worry can be defeated if you use logic to interrupt your thoughts. And you can help counteract sadness or grief if you seek new perspectives on your situation.

See each method to overcome a difficult emotion for more information about it.

Reframe

Once something has triggered an angry response in you, that anger will tend to build on itself and snowball out of proportion. When you feel this happening, take a deep breath and try to reframe the situation. Is there another way to describe it? Are you misinterpreting something?

For example, if a colleague says something upsetting, you can tell yourself your colleague "probably didn't mean it like that." It can also help to ask a third party for an objective opinion on the matter.

Use logic

When you find yourself worrying excessively, you can interrupt the downward spiral of anxiety with logic. You can ask yourself "How realistic is it that my worst fears will actually be realized?" or "What, objectively, are the most probable risks?" It may take some practice to do this effectively, especially if worrying excessively has become a habit for you.

Seek new perspectives

The loss of someone close to you – or of a job, money, or other material items that were important to you – naturally causes sadness. Although allowing yourself some time to grieve or reflect is healthy, this can spiral out of control. It may prompt you to isolate yourself and turn inward, focusing only on sad thoughts.

You can challenge grief by reassessing your situation and trying to interpret it in a different way, or by focusing on what the experience has taught you.

Case Study: Question 1 of 1

Scenario

For your convenience, the case study is repeated with each question.

Rita's close friend at work, Sandra, has just been laid off for frequent absenteeism. Rita is upset because Sandra was one of the few people she got along with at the office. She feels sad that Sandra won't be there anymore, and also anxious about having to make do without her. Rita also feels angry with the management team because she thinks the decision to fire Sandra was unfair.

Consider the scenario and then answer the question that follows.

Question

Match each of Rita's emotions with the statement best suited to countering it. Two of the statements won't be used.

Options:

A. Sadness and a feeling of loss
B. Anger and frustration
C. Anxiety

Targets:

1. "I'm upset now, but I'll adjust eventually. I know I can make other friends here."
2. "To be fair, Sandra wasn't coping. Now she has the chance to find a less stressful job that'll suit her better."
3. "It won't be as lonely as I'm imagining. After all, I can still see Sandra after work and on weekends."
4. "I should stop being ridiculous. It's not like Sandra died or anything."
5. "It's so unfair! My boss always seems to find a way to make things harder for me."

Answer:

Rita can help counter her sadness by seeing it as an opportunity to grow and make new friends. This new perspective will help her focus on the future instead of only on her current sadness.

To defuse her anger and frustration, Rita can reframe the situation by trying to see it from management's point of view, and by focusing on a positive aspect of the situation for her friend.

Rita can help control her anxiety about being without Sandra with logical, rational thoughts about what the situation will really be like.

This harsh admonishment is unlikely to make Rita feel better about the situation. It would be better for her to use gentler, more positive self-talk to regulate her emotional responses.

This blaming statement would only encourage Rita to dwell on the situation further. She should instead try to counteract and challenge her negative thought patterns.

Changing scenery and disclosing emotions

It's important to have variety in your day-to-day life to keep you feeling balanced, healthy, and happy. Too much stress and excitement can take its toll on your health, while too much meditative or serious activity can leave you feeling bored or depressed. Doing something every day that you enjoy or that motivates you and breaks your routine can help you take care of your body and mind.

This is particularly true when you feel mired in strong emotions like anger, worry, or sadness. When this happens, you can try a change of scenery or task to counteract your mood and give yourself a "time out" from your emotion.

This strategy is an especially good one for dealing with stress – which usually accompanies other strong negative emotions. There are limits to the amount of time and effort you can spend counteracting stress. But balancing work and play is key to managing stress and not getting overwhelmed.

What you do to refocus your attention should depend on the emotion you're experiencing. If you're sad or grieving, you should do something to raise your energy levels – like getting some exercise. You could also try lifting your mood with a funny book or motivating movie. If you're angry or worried, you could do something calming like listen to soothing music or seek out a peaceful, natural space to relax in.

If it's not possible to change your physical environment, you can engage in relaxation techniques to change your mental scenery. Take a series of deep, calming breaths while you visualize something that makes you feel at peace.

Again, relaxation techniques are best for anxiety or anger. If you're sad, you should do more motivating activities to keep yourself from dwelling on sad thoughts.

Question

Victor is furious with his boss. He feels she has once again overlooked him for a promotion, although he has been with the company for longer than almost anyone else.

Which strategies are appropriate ways for Victor to deal with his emotional reaction?

Options:

1. Take a peaceful walk along the beach during his lunch break

2. Go to the cinema with a friend after work and watch a comedy

3. Review the situation in his mind to try and figure out why he was overlooked

4. Distract himself by throwing himself into his work to meet a strict deadline

Answer:

Option 1: This is a correct option. A calm, meditative stroll in an area of natural beauty would have a positive effect on Victor and help to soothe his anger.

Option 2: This option is correct. By replacing anger with laughter and doing something enjoyable with a friend, Victor can counteract his emotional response.

Option 3: This is an incorrect option. Dwelling on the situation won't help Victor soothe his frustration. He would do better to get his mind off the situation and calm himself with a more enjoyable activity.

Option 4: This option is incorrect. Although Victor shouldn't lose sight of his deadline, this activity is a stressful one and is unlikely to dissipate his frustration. He should engage in a more calming activity, however briefly.

If someone has upset you, it's important to discuss your emotions to get them out of the way. This is especially true if the person is someone you'll have to deal with regularly, like a colleague. Otherwise, any residual anger will simply rise to the surface next time there's any minor problem in your relationship.

You should disclose your emotions in a clear, calm, and honest way. If you're angry with your colleague for giving you late work, for example, express your anger in language that focuses on you and your feelings, and avoid blaming the other person.

It would be better to say "I get upset when I receive late work, because it makes it hard for me to meet my own deadlines" than "You never do your job properly!" or "It's your fault I'm running late with this project."

In the workplace, it's usually inappropriate to discuss the full depth of a strong emotion like anger. So it's a good idea to allow yourself a cooling-off period before you speak to someone who has made you angry.

You might feel you have a lot to say, but trying to convey all of your emotion can result in a loss of control. You may say or do things you later regret.

Rather than venting at the person, you can record the details of your emotion. This can give you a feeling of release.

Using humor

One way to dispel strong negative emotions is to use humor. Laughter is incompatible with anger, anxiety, or sadness. It also reduces stress. Among other things, humor can help you weather bad situations, lighten your mood, strengthen relationships, smooth over differences, and reframe problems.

However, humor can also be misused. Examples are using sarcasm, ridiculing yourself or others, or concealing your true emotions with supposedly lighthearted behavior or jokes.

Mark, Anita, and Robert use humor in different ways. Select each of these people to find out more about their use of humor.

Mark

Mark has been laid off several times in the past, and, as a result, is deeply insecure about his job. He often makes jokes about being unwanted, but these come off as forced and make his colleagues uncomfortable.

Anita

Anita is secretly jealous of her colleague Gina, who is very talented. After Gina gets promoted, Anita takes many opportunities to crack sarcastic jokes at Gina's expense. Gina eventually starts avoiding her.

Robert

Robert has a gentle and playful sense of humor. People often feel better after spending time with him, because he has the ability to put things in perspective. He uses humor to defuse his work-related anxiety and rarely lets stress get the better of him.

Mark and Anita use humor inappropriately. Mark uses it to cover up his true feelings and Anita uses it to disguise attacks on her colleague. Robert, however, uses humor appropriately. He uses it to defuse his negative emotions rather than to hide them.

Question

While in the cafeteria, one of your colleagues makes a rather spiteful comment about your low productivity. You're hurt and angry that he would say such a thing in front of others and feel a rising urge to argue.

Which are appropriate ways to deal with this emotional reaction?

Options:

1. Give yourself time to cool off and then calmly tell your colleague how you feel

2. Brush off the spiteful comment with a lighthearted joke about your unproductiveness

3. Don't lash out at the time, but later send a detailed e-mail explaining why you're angry

4. Respond in kind by putting your colleague in his place with a joke at his expense

Answer:

Option 1: This option is correct. You should disclose your emotions to your colleague, but give yourself time to cool off before you do to avoid saying something you'll regret.

Option 2: This is a correct option. You can use humor to defuse the situation, as long as you refrain from sarcasm or laughing at your colleague's expense – even if he's upset you.

Option 3: This option is incorrect. Creating a letter may help defuse your anger, but you should refrain from sending it. Explaining the full depth of your emotion probably wouldn't be appropriate.

Option 4: This is an incorrect option. Using humor to belittle other people is inappropriate and will only exacerbate the conflict. If you do use humor, do so to lighten the mood.

Using self-management techniques

Jessica decides to go into the office even though she recently lost a beloved pet. She told herself she should be able to handle herself, but is surprised to find that she's restless and having trouble concentrating. She has withdrawn from her colleagues and is avoiding having to speak to anyone in case she starts crying. She then admits to herself that she's grieving.

Jessica knows from experience she has a tendency to dwell on things and to think all-or-nothing thoughts. She notes she's withdrawing from others and this is just making her sad mood worse. So she takes steps to manage her emotional response before her sadness overwhelms her and she breaks down completely.

Follow along as Jessica takes steps to manage her emotional reaction.

Positive self-talk: Jessica tells herself "Even though I miss him, I know this sadness is temporary. I'll find the strength to get through this."

Reality check: She challenges her negative thoughts by focusing on the good times she had with her dog and what she gained from her time with him.

Change of scenery: Although she doesn't feel like it, at lunch time she deliberately joins her colleagues in the cafeteria, where people are laughing and chatting.

Disclosure: She tells a work friend about her loss, without going into too much detail. Her friend is understanding and supportive, and Jessica immediately feels some weight lift off her shoulders.

Humor: Finally, Jessica listens to jokes around the lunch table and joins in the laughter. She distracts herself from her own sad thoughts.

Jessica relied on self-awareness of her emotional triggers and the physical manifestations of her feelings to identify her emotion. She didn't deny how she felt, but took deliberate, positive steps to manage her emotional reaction and help herself get through it.

Case Study: Question 1 of 2
Scenario

Oliver's immediate boss has asked him to present a report to the company's board members the following week. But Oliver loathes public speaking. Plus, Oliver feels it's unfair he's been picked to do something his boss should rightly have to do.

Oliver can't help obsessing about the upcoming presentation. He is tense, keeps clenching his jaw, is sweating, and is breathing too quickly. It's a familiar feeling for him. He knows he needs to manage his emotional reaction before it overwhelms him.

Answer the questions in the given order.

Question

What emotion or combination of emotions is Oliver feeling?

Options:

1. Anger and anxiety
2. Anxiety only
3. Anger and sadness
4. Anxiety and sadness
5. Anger only

Answer:

Option 1: This is the correct option. Oliver is both angry at his boss for making him do the presentation, and anxious about having to speak to the board.

Option 2: This is an incorrect option. Oliver is anxious, but he's also angry at his boss for what he perceives as unfair expectations of him.

Option 3: This option is incorrect. Although Oliver is angry, he hasn't experienced the kind of loss that would lead to sadness.

Option 4: This option is incorrect. Oliver is certainly nervous about the upcoming presentation, but hasn't experienced the sort of loss that would lead to grief.

Option 5: This is an incorrect option. Oliver is angry with his boss, but he's also anxious about the presentation.

Case Study: Question 2 of 2

Which are examples of actions Oliver can take to manage his emotional reaction?

Options:

1. Go for a long walk by the river that runs near his home
2. Use logic to convince himself that delivering the presentation won't be as terrible as he imagines
3. Tell himself he's an intelligent, capable person and that he'll manage fine
4. Create a long letter explaining his feelings to his boss, but then destroy it without sending it
5. Joke about his nervousness with a trusted work colleague
6. Go straight to his boss's office and vent his anger
7. Cover up his emotions with bravado and sarcasm

Answer:

Option 1: This is a correct option. Oliver can change his scenery and take a peaceful walk in a natural setting to soothe his nerves.

Option 2: This option is correct. Oliver can stop his irrational fears and negative thought patterns by giving himself a reality check.

Option 3: This is a correct option. Oliver can use gentle, positive self-talk to motivate himself and prevent his negative thoughts from getting the better of him.

Option 4: This option is correct. It wouldn't be appropriate to get into an in-depth argument with his boss, so Oliver can defuse his anger by getting his feelings out. But he shouldn't then send his letter.

Option 5: This is a correct option. Using humor can help to counteract Oliver's fear and anger, and reduce the harmful physical effects of stress.

Option 6: This option is incorrect. Venting at his boss will only exacerbate Oliver's anger, and he might say something he later regrets.

Option 7: This is an incorrect option. Oliver should acknowledge his own emotions rather than trying to hide them. Using sarcasm could also damage his relationships.

Giving in to strong emotions like anger, sadness, or anxiety can be disruptive and harmful. A variety of techniques can help prevent emotional breakdowns.

To stop patterns of negative thinking, you can use positive self-talk. A reality check can put a more helpful perspective on a problem. Changing your scenery or task can help to distract you and prevent you from dwelling on an emotion. It's important to disclose strong emotions in a clear, calm way. Finally, using humor can help to lighten a bad mood.

CHAPTER III - USING EMOTIONAL INTELLIGENCE ON THE JOB

CHAPTER III - Using Emotional Intelligence on the Job

Often getting a job done requires objectivity and a focus on the facts. But this doesn't mean you and your colleagues must leave your emotions at the door when you enter the workplace.

Psychologist and author Daniel Goleman performed pioneering work when he identified key competency areas that make up a person's emotional intelligence quotient – commonly known as EQ. These include personal and social areas, related to both awareness and management. This course focuses on the social aspects of EQ – empathy and relationship management.

THE IMPACT OF WORKPLACE EMOTIONS

The impact of workplace emotions

The impact of emotions

To a large extent, your ability to perform the tasks associated with your job is based on your cognitive intelligence. However, your ability to succeed in the workplace is greatly influenced by the impact of emotions – your own and those of your colleagues, coworkers, and others you interact with on a daily basis.

Feelings – which include both emotions and mood – directly affect your outlook, thoughts, and relationships. These, in turn, can dramatically impact your productivity.

Emotions are transient and can be intense. For example, you may dread the thought of giving a presentation, but the emotion dissipates quickly once you get into your stride.

Moods are less intense but longer lasting. For instance, if you enjoy your work, a happy mood colors your days – even if there are some difficult moments.

Emotions at work

Research indicates that emotions in the workplace measurably impact the performance of individuals and groups. Perhaps some of the things you noted about your own emotions follow along with research findings.

- Mild anxiety helps people to think through tricky problems, but intense anxiety prevents people from thinking clearly.

- Anger impels you to take action, but can cause rash decisions, conflict, and misunderstandings.

- Optimism and good humor make it easier to think, work harmoniously with others, and be creative
and persuasive.

- A sober mood aids methodical and accurate analysis, while despondency lowers motivation,
innovation, and cooperation.

Positive and negative feelings have a direct effect on your thinking, decision making, and job satisfaction. They also impact your emotional intelligence and teamwork, and can be self-perpetuating, affecting ongoing moods and emotions in the workplace.

See each factor that feeling can affect for more information about it.

Thinking

Feeling good improves people's ability to understand information, think flexibly, and accurately evaluate complex situations. Optimism and good humor also enhance creativity and teamwork.

Strong negative feelings blunt perceptions, insight, creativity, and your ability to analyze complex information.

However, mild feelings of sadness or anxiety may actually help you think through complex problems methodically.

Decision making

Although you may be unaware of the role your feelings play, you reach better decisions when you feel good. So decision makers' feelings have a measurable effect on an organization's productivity and effectiveness.

A happy person is more persuasive and optimistic, and often plays a significant role in guiding a group's decision making.

Conversely, a sad person may have less influence, but tends to present more considered arguments in favor of a position.

Strong feelings of either optimism or pessimism can skew decision making. Optimists may take unnecessary risks, while pessimists fail to notice opportunities.

Job satisfaction

Job satisfaction is largely based on the percentage of time you feel happy at work. Unhappy workplaces have high staff turnover.

Interestingly, negative interactions with superiors or colleagues are most often the cause of bad feelings at work, rather than interactions with customers or the work itself. This may be due to the contagious nature of feelings.

Because feelings are self-perpetuating, one bad encounter with a boss or colleague can ruin the rest of your day and sour the day for others as well.

People much prefer to be around coworkers who are upbeat and actively seek to work with these individuals.

Emotional intelligence

When you're experiencing negative feelings, you're less able to perceive the emotions of others. This lowers your EQ. The lower your EQ, the poorer your social skills – and the more difficult it becomes to work well in a group.

When you feel good, your social skills and ability to perceive others' emotions improve. This contributes to a cooperative, harmonious, and productive environment.

Teamwork

Good feelings are central to effective teamwork. They make colleagues more willing to help one another and cooperate.

Humor, in particular, stimulates creativity, connects colleagues and makes it easier for them to communicate openly. A spirit of fun and enthusiasm makes teamwork motivating and exciting.

Negative feelings spread quickly through a group, bringing others down. These feelings distract team members from the tasks at hand.

Ongoing feelings and emotions

Feelings and emotions tend to be self-perpetuating. When you experience distress, for example, stress hormones flood your body. These take hours to be reabsorbed. Distressing feelings also evoke further distressing thoughts, which prolong an unpleasant mood.

Additionally, because bad feelings tend to spread to other people, or worsen your ability to get on with others, they are perpetuated in groups. When you're happy, you notice and remember positive aspects of a situation. When you're unhappy, you notice negative details. So feelings give rise to bias and gain momentum.

Question

Which statements illustrate likely effects of particular emotions in the workplace?

Options:

1. Gary's optimism with a new plan makes him tend to overlook its inherent risks

2. Virginia's anger makes it harder for her coworkers to concentrate

3. Carlos's gloomy moods makes him less fun to work with but doesn't stop him from being a good bookkeeper

4. Bella's good cheer means that her department has one of the lowest staff turnover rates 5. Because they tend to laugh a lot, the team members lack motivation to get their job done 6. Barry's extreme pessimism makes him a better decision maker

Answer:

Option 1: This option is correct. Optimistic feelings cause Gary to notice and remember positive information rather than giving equal weight to the negative. This can lead to risky decision making.

Option 2: This option is correct. Anger is disruptive and stressful for others, because negative feelings tend to be contagious – they perpetuate in group settings.

Option 3: This is a correct option. Mildly sad moods can boost caution and accuracy, but they make it harder to get along with others and may also dampen their moods.

Option 4: This is a correct option. Employees, like Bella, who have pleasant interactions with their managers and are mostly happy at work have greater job satisfaction and are less likely to leave their positions.

Option 5: This option is incorrect. Humor enhances group communication and builds a sense of camaraderie, increasing motivation.

Option 6: This is an incorrect option. Barry's extreme pessimism tends to make his colleagues overlook positive information and opportunities, so it has a negative effect on decision making.

Benefits of recognizing emotions

Contrary to what some may think, emotions and moods are anything but trivial in the workplace. Being aware of feelings and understanding their impact can help you identify their role so you can take action to mitigate or enhance their effects on performance.

John is holding a meeting with two of his teammates, Tami and Gail. Follow along as they discuss poor sales figures in the last quarter.

John: You look like you're feeling a little despondent, Tami. Am I right? *John is looking sympathetic.*

Tami: Yes. We've worked so hard and things just aren't getting better. *Tami replies anxiously.*

Gail: Actually, I'm a bit annoyed. I pointed this issue out to Tami two months ago. Why didn't we deal with it then? *Gail responds in annoyance.*

John: OK, I can understand why you'd feel upset about that. Maybe we also need to understand Tami's perspective. What has your experience been over the last few months, Tami? *John asks calmly and sympathetically.*

Tami: I've been working flat out to get our new branding out. I hoped it would boost sales, but it hasn't. I didn't mean to leave you in the dark, Gail. *Tami says anxiously.*

Gail: That's OK. I suppose I didn't understand what you were going through.

John: It sounds like a misunderstanding. We've all been working hard, and it really is going to pay off in the end. Let's put that behind us for now and analyze how market factors have affected the figures. *John suggests with a smile.*

Being able to recognize the impact of feelings in the workplace gives you the ability to read people to understand how productivity is affected, leverage the emotions in a situation, and shape feelings positively rather than allowing the negativity to continue.

See each ability to learn more about the advantages of understanding the impact of feelings in the workplace and how John, because of his understanding, was able to use these advantages to diffuse the conflict between Tami and Gail.

Read people to understand how productivity is affected

It's in your best interest to be aware of the emotional landscape around you. This enables you to read people accurately and understand the forces that affect their performance and decisions.

For instance, by recognizing and attending to Tami's and Gail's feelings, John was able to defuse tension and anxiety to increase productivity.

Leverage emotions

Emotion plays a huge role when teamwork and collaboration are required. So it's important to take advantage of – or leverage – the emotional currents around you. You can do this by matching tasks to current moods.

For example, John suggested they analyze how market factors had affected the results so far. John uses the task to leverage the team's emotions by making them recognize the poor results result from market factors, not from poor work.

Shape feelings positively

Knowledge about others' emotions enables you to shape them in positive ways.

John knew how to soothe his team members' anxieties, and the sense of optimism he initiated should enhance cooperation and improve productivity.

Question

What are the benefits of being able to recognize the impact emotions have in the workplace?

Options:

1. Better understanding of the factors that affect people's performance and decision making

2. The ability to leverage emotions in a way that maximizes performance

3. The ability to shape emotions in positive ways

4. The ability to accurately predict how individuals may react to particular situations

5. Better understanding of how to disconnect emotions from decision making

Answer:

Option 1: This option is correct. People's emotions and moods can affect both their work performance and decision making. Recognizing this can help you understand others and equip you to manage emotions in a way that improves performance and decision making.

Option 2: This option is correct. If you recognize people's emotions and moods, you'll be better able to match people to suitable tasks based on how their feelings are likely to affect their performance.

Option 3: This option is correct. Once you recognize people's emotions, you can take steps to shape them in constructive ways – for example, countering despondency among team members to encourage higher productivity.

Option 4: This option is incorrect. Understanding the impact of people's feelings at work doesn't necessarily enable you to predict how they'll react to particular situations.

Option 5: This option is incorrect. It's not always possible or desirable to ignore emotions during the decision-making process. However, being aware of their impact can help prevent rash decisions.

Emotions and moods can have a profound impact on employees' performance at work. They affect thinking, decision making, job satisfaction, teamwork, and emotional intelligence. They can also be self- perpetuating and influence others in group contexts.

By recognizing and accounting for colleagues' feelings, you can better understand the factors affecting their performance and decision making. You can also leverage emotions to maximize performance and shape emotions in constructive ways to improve productivity.

COMMUNICATING WITH EMPATHY

Communicating with empathy

Empathy
Do you have a colleague who often seems to know how you feel or where you're coming from? If so, this person demonstrates empathy. Empathy is the ability to read, recognize, and thoughtfully consider other people's feelings.

Question
The four areas of competency associated with emotional intelligence can be categorized in a simple matrix, based on whether they're personal or social, and focused on awareness or management.

In which cell of the matrix do you think empathy belongs?

The matrix has two columns, Awareness and Management, and two rows, Personal and Social.

Options:
1. The Social row and the Awareness column
2. The Social row and the Management column

3. The Personal row and the Management column
4. The Personal row and the Awareness column

Answer:

Empathy is social and relates to awareness

Option 1: Empathy is about being aware of how other people are feeling, so it's a social skill that relates to awareness.

Option 2: This cell represents the relationship management competency, which involves social management abilities.

Option 3: This cell represents the personal management competency, which involves managing your own feelings.

Option 4: This cell represents the personal awareness competency, which involves your ability to be aware of your own feelings.

Empathy is the building block for relationship management. It's what gives you the emotional awareness you need to apply your interpersonal skills. It enables you to leverage what other people are feeling and shape people's feelings for the better.

Empathy is a key ingredient in successful relationships. It completes the circuitry that leads to harmony between people – the sense of being on the same wavelength. When you're attuned to your colleagues' feelings, you work better with them – understanding them and reducing conflict.

The characteristics of empathetic colleagues are:
- they listen without interruption or giving advice,
- they read nonverbal cues such as tone of voice and body language,

- they see things from other perspectives, understanding why people feel the way they do, and
- they act with sensitivity, being careful not to hurt, judge, or cut others off when they're speaking.

Empathy and social effectiveness

Because empathy is so important in relationships, it's vital for social effectiveness at work. When you're sensitive to emotional currents around you, you're more likely to say and do the right things. So others enjoy your company and like working with you.

Empathy is particularly important in diverse working environments, which bring together people from different backgrounds and cultures. If you're aware of emotional nuances, you're less likely to misinterpret people who have different ways of doing things.

Demonstrating empathy in the workplace provides a number of important benefits: it fosters an attitude of genuine caring for others

- it feels good and generates productive and satisfying relationships,
- it increases trust and cooperation,
- it builds bridges between people, soothing and dissipating strong emotions so problems can be solved and resistance overcome,
- it's pre-emptive, which means it prevents emotional flare-ups and problems before they begin, and
- it provides information about what's important to people.

What empathy isn't

Telling others what you think they want to hear can come across as insincere. So can automatically offering reassurances or trite aphorisms – for example, "Life's not fair." Each of these mistakes indicates you're not making a real effort to listen to another person.

Showing empathy also doesn't involve trying to solve others' problems for them or sharing facts you think they've overlooked.

Empathy isn't about being saccharine, trying to please people, giving pat answers and reassurances, agreeing with people, or saying whatever you think they want to hear. It's also not about solving people's problems or educating them about the facts.

Question

Which statements accurately describe empathy and its effects in the workplace?

Options:

1. Empathy is a genuine attitude of caring for another person

2. Empathy gives us information about what is really important to someone

3. Empathy is essential to productive and satisfying relationships

4. Empathy makes it easier to solve problems

5. Empathy is about reassuring people

6. Empathy is about finding solutions to problems

Answer:

Option 1: This option is correct. Empathy isn't just about how you behave – it requires an attitude of genuine caring.

Option 2: This option is correct. Empathy helps you to listen actively and learn what really matters to people.

Option 3: This is a correct option. Empathy is key to connecting and relating to people, which is essential for productive and satisfying relationships.

Option 4: This option is correct. When you're aware of other people's feelings, you're more able to understand their needs and adjust accordingly so problem solving becomes easier.

Option 5: This option is incorrect. When you try to reassure people rather than listening to what they have to say, you're not being empathetic.

Option 6: This option is incorrect. Empathy is about being aware of people's feelings, rather than about solving problems they choose to share with you.

Suspending judgment

To use empathy when communicating with others, you can follow this procedure: suspend judgment and access the other person's perspective; identify feelings by paying attention; and communicate your understanding. This doesn't have to be in sequence – each activity may happen simultaneously.

Don't simply jump to conclusions about what someone else is doing or why. Other people have their own values and ways of doing things. Bear in mind that everybody's actions make sense from their point of view. For example, you may be taken aback that a colleague never brings problems to your attention. But perhaps this person is reluctant to approach you and feels this would be presumptuous.

So how do you go about suspending judgment? Cultivate an open, curious, and compassionate attitude.

You need to care about other people and do your best to understand their points of view.

Certain questions are useful tools in suspending judgment and determining another's point of view. See each question for more information about it.

What does this behavior mean to her?

We all come from different backgrounds, so behavior that means one thing to you may mean something quite different to another person.

For example, a colleague always uses your pen without asking and this seem disrespectful to you. For him, this behavior is perfectly reasonable. He thinks pens are a shared office resource.

What options are obvious to her?

It's easier to understand someone else's behavior if you imagine yourself in this person's situation. Ask yourself what options the person feels are available and which would seem best given this person's perspective.

For instance, a colleague is consistently late for work, although she's generally conscientious and hardworking. When you remember she's a homemaker and has responsibilities at home, you get more perspective on her behavior. She may be unaware she can negotiate her work hours and so feel she has no option but to break the rules and get into trouble at work.

How does she view and experience this?

It's important you don't jump to the conclusion that another person's views and feelings are the same as yours. Try to think of what positive reason someone has for behaving in a certain way, rather than assuming the worst.

For example, social occasions might seem like boring time-wasters for you, but vital networking opportunities to someone else.

How would I feel in similar situations?

Asking yourself how you'd feel in a similar situation, or even remembering how you felt in that situation, is very useful. When you do this, you can get real insight and compassion for another person's position.

For example, if your supervisor gets angry when you make a mistake, think about how you'd feel if one of your subordinates was making similar errors. Would you worry about the consequences or that your instructions weren't being taken seriously?

What questions can I ask to understand better?

Think about what questions to ask to gain information and how you can ask these without appearing threatening or judgmental.

Don't disguise a judgment as a question. For example "Please explain your behavior" or "Why did you do it?" aren't helpful requests.

Be genuinely motivated to find out more. To get this right, pay attention to your body language and tone of voice, as well as your words. Useful questions include "Can you help me to understand a bit more?" and "How do you interpret the situation?"

You could also ask people with similar backgrounds how they would feel and react under the circumstances.

Tina has received a scathing e-mail from a colleague, Thom. Follow along as Tina practices suspending judgment.

Tina: It seems from your e-mail you're quite angry with me. Could you help me to understand why? *Tina has open body language.*

Thom: I think that was clear in the e-mail. You're slap-dash in your work and just dump your ideas on my desk, expecting me to figure out what needs to be done. *Thom looks upset, and has closed body language.*

Tina: So is it both my concept drafts and my leaving them on your desk when you're out that's upsetting you? *Tina has open body language and leans forward slightly.*

Thom: Actually your ideas are pretty good, but you don't title and date them. And when you simply leave documents on my desk, it takes me ages to figure out what's going on with them. *Thom has open body language, and seems less upset.*

Tina: I'm sorry. That must be frustrating. I'll include the client name and the date of the draft on each concept pack in future. But what should I do if you're not at your desk? I'm tasked with four different campaigns and I'm really pressed for time. *Tina looks sympathetic.*

Thom: I'm sorry, I wasn't thinking about how much pressure you're under. A name and draft date will be fine for now. When things calm down, you could just send an e-mail to let me know what you've left on my desk. Will that be OK? *Thom looks thoughtful.*

Tina: No problem. I'm glad we've sorted this out. *Tina is smiling.*

Tina approaches the issue without judging Thom's actions first. She genuinely tries to understand his perspective by asking him to help her understand how her behavior is affecting him. Although she initially had a different view of her behavior, she is open to his perspective.

Question

What are ways to get the right perspective when using empathy?

Options:

1. Cultivate an attitude of compassion and caring
2. Remember your colleagues' behavior makes sense to them
3. Ask yourself how you'd feel in a similar situation
4. Ask questions in a genuinely open and non-threatening way
5. Ask others to account for their actions
6. Decide how another person views a situation

Answer:

Option 1: This option is correct. Before you try to see things from someone else's point of view, you should cultivate a compassionate and caring attitude.

Option 2: This option is correct. One way to cultivate the right attitude toward others' behavior is to remember that it makes sense to them.

Option 3: This is a correct option. Asking yourself how you'd feel in someone else's situation can give you valuable insights.

Option 4: This option is correct. You should ask questions without judgment so others feel safe explaining their positions to you.

Option 5: This option is incorrect. Asking others to account for their actions would come across as judgmental and threatening.

Option 6: This is an incorrect option. Although you can come up with ideas about how someone views a situation, you need to confirm your ideas by asking this person.

Identifying feelings by paying attention

To accurately identify what other people are feeling, you need to pay attention to the emotional messages they're sending. So when others are speaking, listen to their words, watch their body language and facial expressions, and notice their tone of voice.

See each tip for identifying other people's feelings to find out more about it.

Listen to the words

Listen attentively and focus on what the speaker is saying. Put down anything you may be busy with and minimize distractions. While you're listening, maintain eye contact and avoid interrupting.

Ask open-ended questions, which elicit more than a simple "Yes" or "No" answer – such as "What do you think about this?"

You can learn a lot about what people feel by listening to the content of what they're saying. However, listening to words only gives a fraction of the information you need. Nonverbal cues provide the rest, and often contain the true message.

Watch body language

People's posture and gestures can speak volumes. Folded arms may signal defensiveness. Leaning forward often shows interest, while leaning back can be a sign that someone's rejecting what you're saying.

What these postures mean should be considered in the context of other cues. Leaning back may mean that someone is actually relaxed and comfortable. Clenched fists, or shoulders held high and forward, may be signs of anger.

Watch facial expressions

Facial expressions convey emotions. A smile and eye contact frequently show interest and cooperation, whereas a diverted gaze and unfriendly expression may indicate disagreement or lack of interest. A person with tight, compressed lips, narrowed eyes, and flared nostrils is probably angry.

Not all facial expressions are easy to read. When someone looks down, for example, she may be feeling sad, worried, guilty, depressed, introspective, or submissive.

Notice tone

The tone of people's voices reflects their emotions. Loud tones could be a sign of anger or stress. Soft tones might indicate uncertainty or shyness. Someone who speaks abruptly may be feeling defensive and rapid speech may show enthusiasm.

People have different patterns of vocal expression, so there's more than one possible interpretation for what feelings are expressed tonally.

Follow along as John tries to find out from Gail how she feels about their new manager.

John: So what do you think of our new manager? *John is maintaining eye contact and leaning forward attentively.*

Gail: He seems very methodical and committed to getting things right. *Gail has her arms folded.*

John: How so? *John looks sympathetic.*

Gail: He wants me to redo my whole sales record! I thought it was already good enough. *Gail is frowning, with her arms open, and gesturing.*

John discovers that their new manager is making Gail feel somewhat threatened by paying careful attention to her words and nonverbal cues. Her arms are initially crossed and her speech is abrupt, indicating defensiveness. He learns why she feels this way by asking an open-ended question.

Question

Gail wants to know what Tami is feeling.

What details should she pay attention to when listening to Tami?

Options:

1. Tami's nostrils are flared
2. Tami speaks softly
3. Tami is leaning back
4. Tami is frowning
5. Tami is neatly dressed
6. Tami speaks with a slight lisp

Answer:

Option 1: This option is correct. Flaring nostrils may indicate anger.

Option 2: This option is correct. Speaking softly may signal shyness or uncertainty.

Option 3: This is a correct option. Tami might be leaning back because she rejects what Gail has been saying.

Option 4: This option is correct. It's possible that frowning indicates anxiety, frustration, or sadness.

Option 5: This option is incorrect. The way Tami dresses isn't an indication of how she is feeling now.

Option 6: This is an incorrect option. Tone rather than other general characteristics of people's voices help tell you what they're feeling.

Communicating understanding

To communicate empathy, you need to acknowledge others' feelings and show you understand these feelings. You also need to demonstrate you're available and supportive, and be nonjudgmental.

See each strategy for communicating empathy for more information about it.

Acknowledge feelings and show understanding

Using your words, vocal tone, facial expression, and body language, you should let other people know you've picked up what they're feeling and understand this.

Examples of useful phrases are "That must be really disappointing," or "I'd also feel disappointed if that happened to me." A look of concern, or a compassionate tone of voice, acknowledges someone's distress.

It's crucial to avoid misinterpreting other's emotions incorrectly. You should also avoid trite or pat statements, which show you weren't really listening.

Demonstrate availability and support

Showing you're available and supportive is key to demonstrating empathy. Even when you don't yet understand what someone is going through, you can still let this person know you're there, care about the situation, and want to help.

You can say this in words or convey caring through your gestures, tone, and facial expressions.

Be nonjudgmental

Don't make statements that judge the speaker, even if you don't agree with what's said. However, pretending to agree is also a mistake. It's insincere and implies that others' opinions aren't important.

You can ask questions to understand better or make open statements that don't imply criticism, such as "Let's look at the situation together," or "Maybe what's happening is..."

It's important not to rush toward finding a solution or offering facts when others are talking about their feelings. This means you aren't really willing to listen.

Follow along as Tami tries to show empathy for Gail after a customer complains about her service.

Gail: I can't believe I made such a stupid mistake. It's so embarrassing. What was I thinking? *Gail looks very upset.*

Tami: Making mistakes can be really embarrassing, but we all get it wrong sometimes. Maybe you'll do better next time. *Tami looks sympathetic, and has open body language.*

Gail: Thanks. *Gail looks sad and embarrassed.*

Tami: If there's anything I can do to help, just say the word. *Tami looks compassionate, and is maintaining eye contact.*

Gail: OK. Thanks for your support, Tami. *Gail looks calmer.*

Tami acknowledges Gail's embarrassment in a nonjudgmental way. But she's too quick to offer reassurances, instead of encouraging Gail to tell her more. Tami lets Gail know she's there for her, so Gail feels comforted. Importantly, Tami conveys warmth and acceptance with her body language, vocal tone, and facial expressions, and doesn't send out conflicting messages.

Question

A colleague tells you how frustrated he feels about being passed over for promotion.

Which responses communicate empathy appropriately?

Options:

1. "I understand why you feel frustrated under the circumstances."
2. "Being passed over isn't a pleasant experience at all."
3. "I'm here for you."
4. "What happened?"
5. "That's so unfair. You really deserve that promotion."
6. "Just try to stay positive about it."

Answer:

Option 1: This option is correct. Your response acknowledges your colleague's feelings and shows understanding of them.

Option 2: This option is correct. Your response validates your colleague's feelings without passing judgment on why he didn't get promoted.

Option 3: This is a correct option. Your answer is supportive and indicates that you're available to listen.

Option 4: This option is correct. Your question is nonjudgmental and indicates your availability to listen.

Option 5: This option is incorrect. With this statement, you're telling your colleague what you think he wants to hear, rather than really empathizing.

Option 6: This option is incorrect. This response is a pat piece of advice – it doesn't demonstrate genuine empathy.

Empathy is the ability to read, recognize, and consider other people's feelings. It's an essential building block for developing relationships and working effectively with others.

To be empathetic, you need to suspend judgment and access the other person's perspective. You do this by setting your assumptions aside, listening compassionately, and approaching conversation with genuine curiosity.

You also need to identify what people are feeling by listening attentively to their words and vocal tone, and watching their body language and facial expressions.

To communicate empathy, you need to acknowledge feelings and show understanding, remain nonjudgmental, and demonstrate your availability and support.

EMOTIONAL INTELLIGENCE SKILLS

Emotional intelligence skills

Using emotional intelligence

Managing relationships requires and incorporates all other areas of competency that make up your emotional intelligence quotient – or EQ. To be competent within the relationship management area, you need to be aware of and able to manage your emotions, and able to recognize and empathize with emotions in others. You then need to use these interpersonal skills to build and maintain successful relationships.

A matrix has two columns – awareness and management – and two rows – personal and social. These create a grid in which the four competency areas associated with emotional intelligence are listed. The self-awareness competency area is personal and relates to awareness, and self-management is personal but relates to management. Empathy is social and relates to awareness, and relationship management is social and relates to management.

The area of relationship management includes many competencies, such as building and using influence, catalyzing change, and showing leadership.

The competencies this topic focuses on are those that build relationships, enhance teamwork and collaboration, and develop people. Each of these requires emotionally intelligent communication.

Emotionally intelligent communication requires reciprocity – a willingness to contribute equally to the emotional component of a relationship. This simply means sharing your own thoughts and feelings when appropriate, and offering the same intensity, openness, and energy to a relationship as the other person.

Emotionally intelligent communication also involves dealing effectively and positively with confrontations. In these situations, be careful to express your feelings and thoughts without blaming or denigrating the person you're speaking to.

When doing this, it's best to avoid expressing your feelings using "you" statements. For example, if you say "You've disappointed me," or "Your behavior makes me angry," the person you're addressing will feel under attack.

By expressing your feelings through "I" statements, you take responsibility for your own feelings without blaming the other person. For example, you can say "I feel disappointed," or "I must admit I feel angry about this."

Communicating during confrontations

To resolve a conflict or handle a confrontation with someone in a positive way, it's particularly important you suspend judgment and access the other person's perspective.

Whenever possible, you should arrange to discuss the issue that's causing conflict, face-to-face and in private. Try to identify the other person's emotions by listening attentively without interrupting, and paying attention to nonverbal cues.

Finally, communicate your understanding of the other person's feelings, providing acknowledgement in a supportive and nonjudgmental way, before expressing your own opinions.

See each strategy for more information on how to use it to resolve confrontations.

Suspending judgment

Before confronting someone, consider the situation from this person's perspective. However, placing yourself in another's shoes is no substitute for actually asking this person's perspective. Use "I" statements to explain the issue from your own perspective and then ask for the other person's perspective.

Examples of useful questions to ask the other person's perspective are "Can you tell me what happened?" "Tell me how you understand this?" and "Could you explain how this happened?"

Identifying emotions

Listening to someone who's angry or upset can be difficult, but pay full attention to what this person is expressing, without interrupting. Encourage the other person to express emotions, without backing away or implying the emotions are inappropriate.

Observations such as "it seems as though you're feeling quite frustrated" can be useful.

Communicating your understanding

Once you've identified the other person's feelings, provide a supportive, nonjudgmental acknowledgement of these feelings.

For example, you might say "I can see how that would upset you," or "That's really frustrating."

When you begin solving a problem after a positive confrontation, collaborate and share your thoughts openly. Avoid dictating or forcing your views on others. For example, avoid statements like "Re-write that report," or "The way to sort this out is to re-write that report." Forcing your views on the other person is disempowering and likely to erode your relationship.

A question such as "What do you think the best solution would be?" empowers the other person by eliciting a response. Similarly, by providing your own view tentatively rather than forcefully, you can provide space for collaboration. For example, you could say something like "I think the solution is to re-write this report – but what do you think?"

When you offer your thoughts in this way, you build relationships, enhance teamwork and collaboration, and help the person you're working with develop.

DEVELOPING SELF-AWARENESS AND EMPATHY

Developing self-awareness and empathy

Mentoring others

To manage relationships effectively, it's important to encourage emotional intelligence in those around you. One way to do this is to model EQ competencies yourself. By behaving with emotional intelligence, you provide an example for others to follow.

A matrix has two columns – awareness and management, and two rows – personal and social. These create a grid in which the four competency areas associated with emotional intelligence are listed. The self-awareness competency area is personal and relates to awareness, and self-management is personal but relates to management. Empathy is social and relates to awareness, and relationship management is social and relates to management.

It's not only emotions that are contagious – attitudes and behaviors are too. When you get it right, people around you raise their EQs, perhaps without even noticing they're doing so.

Simply demonstrating self-control in emotional situations and showing empathy with others in your daily interactions can model good EQ. So modeling is about remaining calm and positive, and about putting your empathy and people skills into practice.

A further way to develop emotional intelligence in others is to ask them the same types of questions you use to improve your own self-awareness. To encourage self-awareness, you should help people question their emotional reactions, triggers, and processes.

See each area for information about how you can encourage self-awareness in others.

Emotional reactions

You can start by asking people to think of particular situations that provoke emotional reactions in them. Ask them to think about the situations and to distinguish carefully between known facts, assumptions, and judgments. Then focus on the facts.

To help others understand their emotional reactions, ask why a situation matters to them, what it's consequences are, and how they're significant.

Then you can go on to questions about what specific feelings the situations evoke and how strong these feelings are.

Emotional triggers

An important aspect of being self-aware is recognizing what triggers specific emotional reactions in you. This can include specific situations, behaviors, assumptions, and judgments.

You can question others to encourage them to identify the triggers for their emotional responses. For example, simply asking something like "What's making you feel this way?" – or perhaps "What types of things typically make you angry?" – can encourage others to consider the sources of their responses objectively.

Emotional processes

Once people know their emotional reactions and triggers, you can ask questions to deepen their awareness of their emotional processes.

Help them to distinguish between the consequences of situations and of the feelings, assumptions, and judgments they provoke. How do these relate to one another? What insights does this give into emotional processes?

Ask people to identify how they respond when triggers are activated and how they think they could better manage these reactions.

A final way to mentor others in emotional intelligence is to help them develop their empathy. You can educate people about empathy. You can also ask questions to encourage empathy in others.

A first step is to encourage others to develop a compassionate, curious, and open attitude. Remind them that everybody's behavior makes sense from their own perspectives. A key goal in empathy is to get insight into what makes another person tick.

Once you've done this, lead others through the same questions you ask yourself to suspend judgment and access other people's feelings and points of view.

Examples of questions you can ask are "What does this behavior mean to the other person?" "What options are obvious to the person?" "How does the other person view and experience this?" "How would I feel in similar situations?" and "What questions can I ask to understand better?"

You should encourage others to further develop questions to find out more about another person's perspective – and remind them to use "I" statements rather than "you" statements when expressing their empathy.

It can also be helpful to use roleplays. Ask people to assume the roles of others and then explain their situations and feelings. Then you can ask and answer questions together and, enriched by the understanding this generates, explore further possibilities.

Question

What examples of questions can you ask others to help them develop their emotional intelligence?

Options:

1. "What situations make you angry?"
2. "What would help you to react better?"
3. "What does this behavior mean to the other person?"
4. "How would you feel if you were in this person's situation?"
5. "Are this person's reasons for behaving in this way legitimate?"
6. "What is the best solution to the problem?"

Answer:

Option 1: This option is correct. Asking people what situations make them angry helps them identify their emotional triggers, which is an important aspect of emotional self-awareness.

Option 2: This is a correct option. Once others recognize their emotions and what triggers them, you can ask questions to encourage them to determine how best to manage their own emotional processes.

Option 3: This option is correct. To encourage others to develop their empathy, you can lead them to consider other people's perspectives and understanding of their own behavior.

Option 4: This option is correct. Asking people how they would feel in another's situation helps them to develop empathy.

Option 5: This is an incorrect option. This question encourages others to judge someone else's behavior, rather than empathizing with this person.

Option 6: This option is incorrect. This question is useful for decision making, but not for developing emotional intelligence.

Managing relationships requires and incorporates all of the other competency areas that make up your EQ – self-awareness, self-management, and empathy. It involves matching your reactions to other people's emotions and building strong relationships, as well as resolving conflict in positive ways.

When you experience a conflict with someone, you should suspend judgment and ask for the other person's perspective. You should also identify and acknowledge this person's emotions. To encourage emotional intelligence in those around you, you can model emotionally intelligent behavior and asking questions that help others develop self-awareness and empathy.

REFERENCES

References
- **The Other Kind of Smart: Simple Ways to Boost Your Emotional Intelligence for Greater Personal Effectiveness and Success -** 2009, Harvey Deutschendorf
- **Put Emotional Intelligence to Work: Equip Yourself for Success** - 2007, Jeff Feldman and Karl Mulle
- **Emotional Intelligence -** 2002, Team Publications, HRD Press
- **Manager's Pocket Guide to Emotional Intelligence -** 2000, Emily A. Sterrett, Ph.D., HRD Press
- **Primal Leadership: Realizing the Power of Emotional Intelligence (A Summary)** - 2002, Daniel Goleman, Richard Boyatzis, Annie McKee, Soundview Executive Book Summaries
- **Emotional Intelligence for Project Managers: The People Skills You Need to**

- **Achieve Outstanding Results** - 2007, Anthony C. Mersino
- **The EQ Interview: Finding Employees with High Emotional Intelligence** - 2008, Adele B. Lynn
- **Put Emotional Intelligence to Work: Equip Yourself for Success** - 2007, Jeff Feldman and Karl Mulle
- **The Emotionally Intelligent Manager: How to Develop and Use the Four Key Emotional Skills of Leadership** - 2004, David R. Caruso and Peter Salovey, Jossey-Bass
- **Emotional Intelligence for Managing Results in a Diverse World: The Hard Truth About Soft Skills in the Workplace** - 2008, Lee Gardenswartz, Davies-Black Publishing

GLOSSARY

Glossary

C

competency - A set of associated skills. For example, emotional intelligence is associated with four main competency areas – self- awareness, self-management, empathy, and relationship management. Each is associated with particular skills.

E

emotional breakdown - A loss of control over one's emotions, resulting in irrational or inappropriate thought and behavior.

emotional intelligence - The ability to process and reason about information related to your emotions and the emotions of others.

emotional intelligence quotient - See EQ.

emotions - Transient and potentially intense feelings.

empathy - In relation to emotional intelligence, the ability to recognize and understand the emotions of others.

EQ - The abbreviation for emotional intelligence quotient; the capacity to identify, assess, and manage your emotions and those of others.

F

feelings - Qualities of consciousness such as happiness, anger, or sadness.

fight or flight response - A natural physical response in which the human body prepares either to confront a threat or flee from it. It's associated, for example, with an elevated heart rate – more oxygen is supplied to the body in preparation for physical exertion. Emotions such as anger can trigger this response even if a person isn't physically threatened.

H

hot button - A word or topic of conversation that evokes a strong, irrational, or inappropriate emotional response in a person.

I

intelligence quotient - IQ

IQ - An acronym for intelligence quotient, a measure of a person's general capacity to reason validly about information.

M

moods - Relatively long-lasting, usually moderate feelings.

N

nonverbal cues - Indications of people's feelings and thoughts that are independent of their words. They can be observed in postures, gestures, facial expressions, and tone of voice.

O

open-ended questions - Questions that elicit more than a simple "Yes" or "No" answer.

P

positive confrontation - Confrontation that has constructive effects and a positive impact on participants' feelings.

R

relationship management - In relation to emotional intelligence, the ability to build positive, productive relationships, to develop people, to manage conflict productively, and to communicate effectively.

S

self-awareness - In relation to emotional intelligence, the ability to recognize your own emotions, their causes, and their impact on your thoughts, actions, and communications with others.

self-control - Another term for self-management.

self-management - In relation to emotional intelligence, the ability to control or regulate your emotions, rather than reacting instinctively.

T

tone - Vocal inflections, such as pitch and volume, to express emotions.

www.ingramcontent.com/pod-product-compliance
Lightning Source LLC
Chambersburg PA
CBHW020919180526
45163CB00007B/2809